Brave on Purpose

LEADING TEAMS WITH COURAGE, CONNECTION, AND A WHOLE LOT OF HEART

Samantha Hamilton

Principal Principles Publications

United States of America

Samantha Hamilton/Principal Principles Publications

502 Breckenridge Street

Neosho, MO 64850

Thebarefootprincipal.com

Ordering Information:

Quantity sales. Special discounts are available on quantity purchases by corporations, associations, and others. For details, contact the "Special Sales Department" at the address above.

Brave on Purpose/Hamilton.-1st ed.

Paperback ISBN: 979-8-9987351-0-3

eBook ISBN: 979-8-9987351-1-0

Table of Contents

Dedication

To Brandon—
My steady place, my best friend, and my safe landing. Your patience, strength, and unwavering belief in me have carried me through the hardest chapters and the brightest ones too. Thank you for being my rock through leadership, motherhood, and book deadlines.

To Maggie, Tucker, and Abbie—
Thank you for sharing me with so many other kids over the years. You are my why, my joy, and my greatest adventure. I love you more than all the Christmas trees in the world.

To my mom and dad—
Thank you for showing me what it means to lead with love, to teach with passion, and to never stop believing in the power of education.

To my sisters—
We may walk different paths, but we are forever connected by strength, story, and shared beginnings. I'm grateful for the roots that shaped us and reminded me that, no matter what, family is everything.

To my inner circle—Those who believe in me
You know who you are. Thank you for the late-night texts, the reminders to keep going, and the grace you give me when I'm running on fumes. I couldn't do this without you.

To my team—past and present—
Thank you for letting me lead, learn, and love alongside you. Every shared hallway, hard day, and joyful win helped shape this story.

To Autumn—

You were once my teammate, but have become a leader I admire, a mentor I trust, and a friend I treasure. I hope to be half the educator you are one day. Thank you for sharpening me, challenging me and standing beside me. Always.

To those who didn't believe in me—

Thank you, too. Your doubts became my drive. Your resistance made me resilient. You helped build this version of me, and I'm grateful.

And most of all, to God—

Thank You for authoring every chapter long before I knew the plot. For opening doors I didn't knock on, calming storms I couldn't see coming, and weaving purpose into every pause. All glory to You.

Brave on Purpose is a love letter to educators in the trenches-an invitation to lead with clarity, courage, big heart, and a little sparkle.

Part 1:

The Inside Work of Leadership

Lead Anyway: A Note From the Edge

Let me be honest: leadership is not for the faint of heart.

It's beautiful and brutal. Fulfilling and exhausting. Thrilling and terrifying—all on the same day. (Or let's be real... the same hour.)

But if you've picked up this book, I'm guessing you already know that.

You're in the trenches. You've got the battle scars.

And you're still staying in it, even when it's hard.

That says something about you.

This book is for those who lead from the heart, even when it hurts. It's for those who don't just want to get through the day—they want to make it matter. Whether you're a first-year principal, an aspiring administrator, a teacher-leader figuring it out as you go, or someone bold enough to take on school culture with grit and grace—I wrote this for you. Because I've been where you are, and I know how lonely leadership can feel when you're standing at the edge. I've led through chaos and crisis—through literal and figurative tornadoes.

I've made mistakes, course-corrected, and kept going.

I've cried in my car and danced in the hallways. I have fought for a school culture that didn't just survive—but came alive. Along the way, I learned this: leadership is not about power or perfection. It's about people. And the courage to lead with purpose, even when the path is anything but straightforward.

So, no, this book is not a list of leadership buzzwords or a glorified checklist of what "great leaders" do. This is the real stuff. The late-night, early-morning, middle-of-the-chaos stuff. It's part memoir, mirror, manual, and all heart. You'll find stories that might sound like yours. We were never meant to lead from the center.

We were meant to lead from the edge.

That's where the risk is. That's where the growth is.

And if you're brave enough to step out there, I promise—there's something powerful waiting on the other side.

WE WERE MEANT LEAD FROM THE EDGE.

Something worth building. Something worth becoming.

Let's do this. Together.

CHAPTER 1

The Mindset of a Courageous Leader: Stepping Up in the Storm

"HARDSHIPS OFTEN PREPARE ORDINARY PEOPLE FOR AN EXTRAORDINARY DESTINY." – C.S. LEWIS.

Stepping Up in the Storm: Leading Through the Aftermath of a Tornado

On April 4, 2017, a tornado destroyed our elementary school in a matter of moments. Standing in the rubble with my team, the weight of unanswered questions pressed in:

Where would our students go?

How would we rebuild?

How could I lead when everything had fallen apart?
But in that moment, one thing became clear—there was no time for despair.

I wasn't alone. Not even close. Yet the weight of leadership still pressed down hard. I had 320 students, 25 teachers, and an entire community looking to us for direction. It was time to step up.

Even with support all around me, the responsibility felt overwhelming. That's one of the most complex truths about leadership—it can feel incredibly heavy, even when you're not carrying it alone. I had mentors, friends, and colleagues walking beside me, but there's something uniquely isolating about being the one everyone looks to for answers.

In those moments, I leaned on resilience and the example of others who led with heart. My superintendent modeled servant leadership with grace and steadiness. He took a chance on me, and I'm forever grateful to have learned beside such a steadfast leader. So much of what I believe about leadership was formed in those early, uncertain days—when I was being led well at a time when I didn't even know how to lead myself.

We were surrounded by kindness—advice, donations, time, hands, and shoulders to lean on. What I learned in those days is that leadership in crisis isn't about doing it alone. It's about leaning on those around you, learning from those who came before you, and finding the collective strength to rise again.

The Impossible Task: Rebuilding a School

Since our students couldn't return to a destroyed building, we had to create a new one—fast. We had only three school days and a weekend to do this.

We reopened the school in just five days—that number still stuns me. We had to reimagine everything: transportation routes, classroom assignments, cafeteria setups, signage, traffic flow, materials, supplies—everything. Teachers rolled carts through unfamiliar halls. Students sat in mismatched desks. Our whole team learned from uncertainty, stress, and deep fatigue.

And yet—we showed up.

It wasn't pretty, but it was powerful. Somehow, we pulled off what most would call impossible through sheer will and a shared purpose. We weren't just opening a building but creating a sense of safety, normalcy, and hope in the middle of chaos. That was the real work. And it changed me forever.

Leadership doesn't always come with a guidebook. Sometimes, it looks like duct tape, sheer grit, and praying no one notices how close you are to falling apart. But it also looks like people are showing up for one another—sleeves are rolled up, hearts wide open.

We did more than rebuild a school—we rebuilt belief.

Leadership Lessons from the Rubble

The tornado didn't just shake our foundation—it reshaped my understanding of leadership.

Before the storm, I thought leadership was about having the answers. I thought it was about being polished, prepared, and always ready with a plan. But in the days that followed the storm, I learned something much more profound: leadership is about being present when there are no answers. It's about standing in the literal or figurative rubble and choosing to keep showing up anyway.

There was no playbook, checklist, or neatly packaged district protocol. We had raw urgency and a community willing to piece it together with grit, heart, and hope.

I didn't have all the right words, and I didn't know how to comfort everyone, but I could stand beside them and say, "We'll figure it out together." In those moments, I realized leadership isn't about being the strongest voice in the room but the most present. When people are scared or overwhelmed, they don't need a superhero. They need someone who will listen, someone who will hold space for the hard, someone who chooses hope.

There's a difference between pressure and presence. Pressure says: "You better get this right." Presence says: "You don't have to do this alone."

And our people showed up. Again and again.

Teachers brought snacks for students who had lost everything. One counselor showed up to comfort kids even though her belongings and office had been ripped apart. Staff members sorted supplies and set up makeshift classrooms, often with tears in their eyes and laughter on their lips—because we knew if we didn't laugh, we might fall apart. Parents volunteered to clean, organize, and simply sit beside us as we figured it out.

In the middle of the mess, I saw the purest form of leadership: shared responsibility and unwavering care.

The storm revealed who we were. But more importantly, it revealed who we were becoming.

So I checked in, listened, reassured, and reminded them that we were doing this together. And yes, we made "So Happy Together" our theme, complete with a '60s vibe and more tie-dye than you can imagine!

When Nothing Feels Normal

The school day finally arrived. Our students returned—not to the familiar comfort of their classrooms but to a patchwork of barely functional learning spaces.

First, second, and third graders were crammed into a gymnasium, with file cabinets and donated bookshelves serving as makeshift walls. Fourth graders were relocated to a FEMA shelter inside another elementary school, where they tried to adjust to a culture and community that didn't feel like home. Kindergarteners and preschoolers scattered across two more unfamiliar buildings, doing their best to find safety in spaces that weren't built for them.

And then—testing season hit.

State-mandated assessments, the high-stakes kind that shapes perception and funding, were now being administered in whatever spaces we could find: conference rooms, storage closets, and hallways. Students moved from one space to another, following availability instead of routine. There was no consistency, predictability, or peace.

Music echoed through thin walls. Doors slammed. Footsteps echoed. Strangers wandered in and out. Focus was hard to come by. Teachers tried their best to shield students from the chaos, but the exhaustion was etched on their faces.

Still—we showed up. Still—we taught. Still—our students tried.

This wasn't resilience wrapped in a bow. It was gritty, messy, imperfect perseverance. It was educators refusing to let conditions define expectations. It was students adapting in ways adults rarely give them credit for.

We weren't thriving yet, but we were standing. And sometimes, that's enough.

What the Tornado Taught Me About Leadership

Looking back, I realize that experience didn't just test me as a leader—it reshaped me. It wasn't just about surviving a crisis. It was about growing through it.

Resilience isn't always loud or heroic. Sometimes, it's silent and scrappy. It looks like showing up the next day—not with all the answers, but with the courage to stay in it. Leadership isn't about having the perfect plan but adapting when that plan falls apart. I learned that no matter how broken things seem, we can rebuild, reimagine, and rise again.

That season didn't last forever, but it was real and left its mark. I didn't stand alone. I was held up by a village of people who refused to let me sink. And in that, I discovered a truth I'll never forget:

The strength of a school isn't measured by how well it functions when things are easy. It's measured by how well it holds together when everything is hard.

Another lesson was just as humbling: People must come before the process.

We were so focused on solving the logistical crisis—finding classrooms, moving supplies, and getting back to "normal"—that we didn't stop to care about the emotional toll it was taking on our people. We rebuilt a school but didn't take enough time to rebuild our teachers and students.

If I could go back, I would create more space for grief, more time to process, and more permission to pause. I would've told my team,

"You don't have to be okay right now. You just have to be honest."
That realization led me down a deeper path—into the study of
trauma, the adult brain, and how crisis disrupts our sense of safety
and self-worth.

Finally, and maybe most importantly, I learned this: A storm can't
destroy culture.

A building is just a structure. A school is its people. The tornado took
our walls but didn't take our commitment, belief, or love for our
students. When everything fell apart, we didn't let go of each other.
And that's what carried us through.

The Silver Lining: A Fresh Start

What once felt like an impossible task became a transformational
journey.

The adversity we faced didn't just challenge us—it refined us. It
made us stronger, closer, and more innovative than ever. And today,
that school stands not just rebuilt but reimagined—anchored in
purpose and possibility.

Two years after the tornado, we opened the doors to a brand-new
campus designed intentionally for student-centered learning.
Flexible seating, collaborative spaces, natural light, and integrated
technology—every inch of that building was crafted with kids in
mind. It is a place where learning feels alive, creativity is welcomed,
and students and teachers are encouraged to think differently.

But the most powerful shift wasn't in the architecture. It was in the
mindset.

During our months in temporary classrooms, we experimented,
adapted, let go of old assumptions, and tried new ways to engage

students. In the mess, we discovered momentum. Our resilience became our strength, and that strength became our story.
This wasn't just survival. It was leadership at the edge of uncertainty.

And that edge—that sacred, uncharted space between disaster and hope—is where authentic leadership begins.

Mirror Moment: How Do You Lead in a Storm?

Not every leader will face a tornado.
But every leader will face a storm.

Maybe yours won't come with shattered windows and toppled trees—but it will arrive in unexpected challenges, heartbreaking decisions, or moments when the ground beneath you no longer feels steady. It might be a conflict that divides your team, a loss within your school community, or a change that shakes the foundation of everything familiar.

When that moment comes—and it will—how will you lead?

Will you be the calm in the chaos? The steady voice reminding your people they are capable, even when they're weary? Will you choose to see the glimmers of good, even in the darkest moments?

Here's what I know: storms are inevitable. But so is the strength that can rise from them—if we lead with clarity, compassion, and courage. The storm may shake us, but it doesn't have to break us.

How you show up in those moments will define far more than the crisis itself—it will shape your culture, credibility, and legacy.

Practical Strategy: Reframe Setbacks as Stepping Stones.

Think about a challenge you've faced recently.
How did you initially view it?
What did you learn?

Write down one lesson you want to carry with you into future challenges. And always remember: The storm doesn't define you—how you rise from it does.

Setbacks are not roadblocks; they are redirections.
The most effective leaders don't just endure challenges—they use them as fuel for growth, creativity, and transformation.

Here's a step-by-step strategy to help you reframe setbacks as stepping stones to something greater:

1. Shift Your Perspective – Ask Better Questions

When a setback hits, your instinct might be to ask, "Why is this happening to me?" Instead, shift your thinking with questions like:

- "What can I learn from this?"
- "How might this make me stronger as a leader?"
- "What opportunity is hidden in this challenge?"

That mental shift changes everything.

When we lost our school in the tornado, I could have fixated on everything we'd lost—classrooms, materials, routine. (Believe me, it was tempting.)

But instead, I asked:
- What could we do differently—things we never would've considered before?

- How might we use this to reimagine our learning spaces?
- What lessons in resilience could we model for our students?

Those new questions redirected my energy from grief to growth.

2. Identify the Silver Linings

Every disruption, no matter how disorienting, holds potential. Your role as a leader isn't just to weather the storm—it's to scan the horizon and help your team see what's still possible.

Disruption can lead to innovation—if you're willing to let go of what used to be. Ask yourself:
- What systems weren't serving us well anyway?
- What routines or mindsets had we outgrown?

Sometimes, chaos clears the path for reinvention.

After the tornado, our team tried everything—teaching in gyms, co-teaching across grades, rethinking routines, repurposing spaces. At first, it felt like duct-taped survival. But eventually, something remarkable emerged: creativity, flexibility, collaboration. What started as triage became the seed of transformation.

Even failure has something to teach us. It shines a light on what isn't working and reveals where leadership needs to stretch and evolve. When things fall apart, don't waste the rubble. Ask:

- What is this moment trying to teach me?
- What would I do differently next time?

Strong leaders mine failure for wisdom—not shame.

3. Let Adversity Build Connection

There's nothing like a shared struggle to forge a lasting connection.

Some of the deepest bonds in our school were formed after disaster struck. We saw each other in raw, honest ways. We grieved together, laughed at absurd mishaps, and celebrated the tiniest wins. There's something sacred about surviving something hard as a team—it creates trust and empathy that can't be manufactured any other way.

Yes, the storm left a mess. But buried in that mess was the opportunity to lead differently—if we were brave enough to look for it.

The Work Matters

And I'll be honest with you—there were moments I fell.
Leading from the edge sounds bold and brave.
But sometimes, the edge crumbles.

Sometimes, fear wins. Sometimes, you lose your footing. I have—more than once.

But I've learned this: failure doesn't disqualify you from leadership. Giving up does.

Reflection, vulnerability, and reconnecting to your why are how you rebuild.

To every leader reading this:
You are capable. You are strong. You will rise.

Whether your storm is literal—tearing down the walls around you—or internal, shaking the confidence within you, know this:

Leadership isn't about having every answer.

It's about taking the next step, even when the path is unclear.

It's about leading with heart, lifting others as you climb, and believing in the power of resilience forged through hardship.

So keep going even when it feels impossible, doubt whispers, and no one's clapping.

> **LEADERSHIP ISN'T ABOUT HAVING EVERY ANSWER. IT'S ABOUT TAKING THE NEXT STEP, EVEN WHEN THE PATH IS UNCLEAR.**

Keep showing up. Keep leading with conviction. Because your work matters.

Leadership Soundtrack: Stepping from the Storm

Track 1: "Brave" – Sara Bareilles

"Say what you wanna say / And let the words fall out / Honestly, I wanna see you be brave..."

The storm reveals your strength. But what comes next reveals your heart.

After the chaos settles, leadership shifts—from holding everything together to holding space for healing.

This is where courage becomes connection. And that connection is the foundation of lasting culture.

In the next chapter, we move from rubble to relationship.

Because while a crisis can steady a team, only love sustains one.

CHAPTER 2

Leading with Heart

"PEOPLE DON'T CARE HOW MUCH YOU KNOW UNTIL THEY
KNOW HOW MUCH YOU CARE."—JOHN C. MAXWELL.

Rethinking Leadership

I used to believe leadership was about knowledge, strategy, and authority. I'd be an effective leader if I had the correct answers, set clear expectations, and stayed ahead of the curve.

But I was wrong.

Over time, I learned that relationships—not authority—are the heartbeat of leadership. Once I truly understood that, everything changed.

The Moment That Changed Everything

During the 2021–22 school year, my world shifted.

What began as a call to help students in crisis turned into something we never expected—we welcomed four children into our home. Overnight, we went from a family of five to a family of nine. It was a crash course in foster care—not just the system on paper but the lived reality—the chaos, the heartbreak, the courage. And it cracked something open in me.

It was a complete culture shock. I thought I understood the reality of foster care. After all, I had worked with children from complex backgrounds for years. But living it? Being deep in the trenches of the child welfare system? That was an entirely different kind of knowing.

Before this experience, I'll admit—sometimes, I assumed the worst. I thought parents in crisis chose not to do better, that neglect was a choice, that dysfunction came from apathy, not from deep-rooted trauma or lack of support. If families cared enough, they wouldn't be in these situations.

I was wrong.

That year opened my eyes and softened my heart in ways I can't explain. I began to see clearly that many families aren't choosing dysfunction—they're doing their best with what they have. Cycles of poverty, abuse, and instability don't break without help, and often, people never have a chance to learn a different way.

This wasn't just a personal shift—it was a leadership shift. If we, as schools and communities, want our students to truly thrive, then we can't just teach them from 8 to 3.

To make a lasting impact, we must reach beyond the school day— into homes, hearts, and communities.

Beyond the 8-3: Building Trust, One Relationship at a Time

This shift in perspective didn't stay personal—it sparked something much bigger. It led to action.

If we wanted kids to thrive, we had to do more than implement behavior plans and academic interventions during school hours. We had to support the whole family. It wasn't enough to care from 8 to 3—we needed to show up beyond the bell.

That's how the "**Beyond the 8–3**" initiative was born.

We knew we couldn't do it alone, so we invited community partners, churches, and local agencies to help us fill the gaps—to extend support beyond our walls and into the homes of the families we served.

My team was extraordinary, tireless, compassionate, and all-in. They gave their energy, time, and hearts to build something meaningful—not because it was required, but because they believed in the kids behind the data and the families behind the stories.

Family Wellness Nights: Meeting Families Where They Are

The initiative's first and most transformational piece was Family Wellness Nights—monthly, invite-only gatherings designed to build trust, offer support, and foster connection without judgment, comparison, or fear.

We intentionally invited families we knew needed deeper support—those involved with foster care, referred by counselors or teachers, enrolled in the Backpack Program, or engaged in Tier 2 or Tier 3 behavior supports. These were families often overlooked or misunderstood—ones carrying invisible loads.

Each event followed a warm, welcoming structure. Families were greeted with a hot, home-cooked meal provided by local churches or community volunteers. We served it on real plates with actual silverware—not because it was fancy, but because it signaled something deeply human: **you matter.**

Before splitting into groups, parents were invited to tell their children one thing they were proud of—a simple but powerful practice that nurtured connection and planted seeds of affirmation. Then, we broke into groups: parents received practical tools and strategies while students engaged in hands-on activities around the same topic.

We closed the evening by bringing everyone back together for reflection, shared learning, and a take-home resource that extended the conversation beyond the event.

These nights weren't just programs—they were bridges. Between school and home. Between stress and support. Between intention and impact.

The First Wellness Night: A Small Step, A Big Impact

Our very first Family Wellness Night focused on a topic that might seem small—dental health.

But for many of our families, this was a real and often overlooked challenge.

We invited a local dentist to lead an interactive session for students, turning lessons about brushing and flossing into a fun, engaging experience. Meanwhile, adults met with professionals from a local care facility who provided valuable guidance and resources to support their children's dental hygiene at home.

At the night's end, each family was left with more than just a new toothbrush and toothpaste for every household member. They left full from a hot, home-cooked meal. They left seen, heard, and supported. Most importantly, they left knowing they were not alone. The feedback was immediate and powerful. One parent told us, "For the first time, I felt like the school saw me. Like I belonged here." Another said, "I didn't feel judged. I felt helped."

That night shifted something. It started small, but it sparked something big. Families wanted to come back. They looked forward to the next gathering. And we knew—this was more than an event. It was the beginning of something transformational.

Building a Sustainable Future

As Family Wellness Nights grew, so did our vision.

We selected new themes each month based on parent feedback, teacher observations, and real-time student needs. We addressed medical care and access to essential health resources. We tackled home organization and cleanliness, teaching kids to take ownership of chores and daily routines. We explored positive discipline and parenting strategies—setting boundaries, encouraging healthy behavior, and deepening parent-child relationships.

We covered practical life skills like cooking, cleaning, and budgeting. We introduced digital safety, helping parents navigate online spaces with confidence. And we didn't shy away from tough topics like body safety and personal hygiene, equipping families with the tools to care for themselves and each other.

Each session was designed to do more than inform—it was meant to transform, spark confidence, build capacity, and strengthen the partnership between home and school.

To encourage consistent participation, we offered a simple incentive: families who attended at least seven of nine events would receive a catered steak dinner from a local restaurant.

But the real reward wasn't steak—it was trust.

Walls began to fall, conversations deepened, and relationships formed. We didn't just have families attending; we had families returning because, for the first time, they felt like they belonged. And that's where lasting change begins.

The Power of Relationships in Leadership

Looking back, I realize this shift—this entire initiative—wasn't just a new program. It was a new kind of leadership, a return to what matters most.

Because, at its core, education is not just about academics. It's about people.

Leadership isn't about having the loudest voice or the sharpest plan. It's not about authority. It's about service. It's about showing up—not to command, but to connect.

I no longer believe effective leadership is defined by having all the answers. It's defined by presence, building trust, and walking alongside others in their journey.

Authentic leadership doesn't come from standing at the front of the room, giving directions. It comes from sitting at the table, asking questions, listening, learning.

It comes from seeing the person behind the performance, the story behind the struggle.

And it comes from loving your people enough to lead with heart—even when it's hard.

Mirror Moment: How Do You Lead with Heart?

Leadership isn't about authority—it's about relationships. It's built on trust, connection, and the ability to inspire others toward a shared vision.

LEADERSHIP ISN'T ABOUT AUTHORITY —IT'S ABOUT RELATIONSHIPS.

So pause for a moment and ask yourself:

- How am I building trust with those I lead?
- Do people feel seen, heard, and valued in my presence?
- Am I demonstrating empathy before expecting accountability?

Leadership begins with presence. It begins with how you make people feel when you walk into a room.

Do you listen more than you speak?
Do you make space for stories—not just schedules?
Do people breathe easier or brace themselves when you enter the room?

Now, think about someone who shaped the way you view leadership. A teacher. A mentor. A coach. A family member. What made them unforgettable? What did they do that made you feel capable, uplifted, and safe?

Now, ask: How can I become that kind of leader?

Write down three simple things you can do today to lead with the same heart, presence, and impact.

Practical Strategy: 3 Ways to Build Trust with Staff and Students

1. Show Up and Be Present

One morning, I walked into a kindergarten room just to say hi—tied twelve tiny shoes, and joined a dance party during circle time. That three-minute moment? The teacher later told me it was the first time she'd felt truly seen all week.

Presence doesn't require a clipboard. It requires intention.

For staff: Stop by classrooms just to check-in. Ask how they're doing—really. Show up when it's hard, not just when it's scheduled.

For students: Be visible at recess, cafeteria, and dismissal. Learn names. Ask questions. Celebrate them—even for little things.
Trust is built in the small, ordinary moments—not just the big, public ones.

2. Listen More Than You Speak

I once asked a student how her day was going. She shrugged and said, "You don't want to know." So I sat down and said, "Try me." That five-minute hallway pause turned into a mentorship that lasted all year.
Trust starts when people feel heard.

For staff: Create regular check-ins, host listening sessions, use anonymous surveys, and actually respond to the feedback. Don't assume you know what they need—ask.

For students: Go beyond the "How are you?" Take the time to dig deeper. "What's on your mind today?" "What do you need more of in class?" "What's something I don't know about you yet?"

When people feel heard, they feel valued. And when they feel valued, they begin to trust.

3. Follow Through on Your Word

A teacher once asked me to order stools for her small group area. It wasn't urgent, but I said I would. Weeks later, when they arrived, she smiled and said, "Honestly, I didn't think you'd remember."

It's never just about the stools.
It's about the promise.

For staff: Keep your word. Follow up even when it's small, especially when it's small. It builds credibility faster than a thousand mission statements.

For students: Be honest, fair, and consistent. If you say something matters, show them it does.

Trust isn't built overnight. It's built in the repeat. Over and over again.

Leadership is a Relationship

At its core, leadership is not about authority—it's about relationships.
And relationships are built on trust.

So start there.
Show up. Listen. Follow through.

Because when people know you care, they'll go with you anywhere—even into the unknown.

Vulnerability unlocks trust.
But when that trust is nurtured over time, something deeper forms: a culture where people feel seen, safe, and part of something bigger than themselves.

As we move into the next chapter, we zoom out—from the personal work of leading with heart to the collective work of building a school culture where connection, care, and purpose are not accidental... they are intentional.

Leadership Soundtrack: From Compassion to Conviction

Track 2: "Home" – Phillip Phillips
"Just know you're not alone / 'Cause I'm gonna make this place your home."

Vulnerability is the beginning—but belonging is the goal.

Leadership isn't just about leading people forward.
It's about making them feel like they belong along the way.

In the next chapter, we step into shaping a culture that lasts—one where care is baked into the system, not just sprinkled on top.

Because great leadership doesn't just move people.
It holds them.
And it builds a place where they want to stay.

CHAPTER 3

Know Who You Are: Leading with Core Values

"IF YOU DON'T STAND FOR SOMETHING, YOU'LL FALL FOR ANYTHING."- MALCOLM X.

The Foundation Leadership

Leadership isn't about popularity. It's not about doing what's easiest or making decisions that please everyone.

True leadership is anchored in values—the non-negotiable principles that hold you steady in a storm and guide you when the road ahead is unclear. The strongest leaders aren't the ones who bend to pressure or avoid discomfort. They are the ones who stand firm in their convictions—even when it's hard.

YOUR VALUES ARE YOUR ANCHOR—LEAD WITH CONVICTION, NOT CONVENIENCE.

A Time I Had to Stand Firm in My Values

There was a time in my leadership when I had to make a tough call that involved shifting resources midyear in a way that disrupted routines and drew a lot of criticism.

It would've been easier to avoid the heat.
But I knew what was right.
I knew my responsibility to students outweighed the temporary comfort of keeping things the same.

I remember the weight of that decision. The isolation that came with it. But I also remember the clarity—the deep, gut-level knowing that I acted with integrity and purpose.

Leadership isn't about being liked.
It's about being respected for the integrity of your choices.

That experience cemented something in me:
When you lead with authenticity and a clear sense of purpose, the right people will stand with you—even when it's hard.

The Ripple Effect of Authentic Leadership

Leadership isn't about authority—it's about influence.
It's not about control—it's about integrity.
The best leaders don't demand compliance; they inspire belief.

When leaders model honesty, humility, and a clear sense of purpose, their influence ripples out—shaping school culture, staff morale, and student success.

I think of Satya Nadella, CEO of Microsoft, who didn't transform the company by enforcing stricter policies or tightening control. He changed it by listening, leading with empathy, encouraging innovation, and modeling vulnerability. He built trust, and that trust revitalized an entire culture.

That's the power of authentic leadership. And it always begins with one thing: self-awareness.

When you know your values—and align your actions with them— you create a space where others feel safe doing the same. That alignment becomes your credibility. And that credibility becomes your impact.

The Power of Servant Leadership

One of the most defining leadership values in my journey is servant leadership, a concept introduced by Robert Greenleaf in 1977. At its core, it means this: the leader's primary role is to serve, to put others first, to build trust, not authority, and to create shared ownership, not top-down control.

I experienced the power of this firsthand when our school faced personnel transitions.

Instead of making all the decisions behind closed doors, I invited my staff into the process. We held open forums, and every teacher and team member had a voice. And something remarkable happened— people didn't just tolerate the hard choices; they contributed to them. They brought creative, compassionate solutions because they felt trusted and included.

We found a way forward—one that minimized the impact on students and strengthened our team's culture.

That experience didn't just solve a financial problem.
It solidified something in me: Leadership is most potent when it lifts others up, not when it keeps them in line.

Servant leadership doesn't mean surrendering accountability or abdicating responsibility—it means recognizing that leadership is a relationship, not a position. It means believing people will rise to the occasion when they feel seen, valued, and trusted to help shape the outcome.

The Power of Self-Awareness and Vulnerability

Leadership takes courage—but not the kind that pretends to have it all together. Real courage is vulnerability. It's the strength to admit what you don't know. It's leading through uncertainty with honesty, humility, and openness.

Brené Brown's research in Dare to Lead (2018) is clear: vulnerability builds trust. She shares the story of a hospital administrator who admitted uncertainty instead of pretending to have the answers during a crisis and chose to problem-solve with the team. That act didn't erode his credibility—it deepened it. His transparency became a bridge to collaboration.

I've experienced this, too.

There have been moments when I've felt the pressure to appear unshakable. But I've learned that showing vulnerability doesn't weaken your leadership—it humanizes it. Saying, "I don't have the answer, but I'll figure it out with you," creates space for shared ownership and trust.

Self-awareness—knowing your strengths, triggers, and blind spots—is essential for leading well. Leaders who lack it often lead through ego or fear. But leaders who reflect, recalibrate, and grow... create environments where others feel safe to do the same.

Even leaders at the highest levels struggle. In Lean In (2013), Sheryl Sandberg talks openly about battling imposter syndrome—despite her title, achievements, and influence. Her honesty reminds us that self-doubt doesn't disqualify you. It invites you to grow.

Great leaders don't hide their uncertainty.
They lead through it—with authenticity and reflection.

The Courage to Embrace Failure

One of the most essential leadership values I hold is resilience—the ability to see failure not as a verdict but as a teacher.

In her 2008 Harvard Commencement address, J.K. Rowling spoke about hitting rock bottom. That moment, she said, gave her the clarity to focus entirely on what mattered most: her writing. The failure didn't break her—it became the foundation for her success.

That message stuck with me.

Because leadership isn't about never falling—it's about getting back up with more clarity and compassion than before.

I've learned that failure is not a sign of incompetence. It's a sign of effort. The most effective leaders don't fear falling—they embrace it, learn from it, and use it as fuel.

At the heart of every genuinely grounded leader is a set of core values—deep roots that keep you steady when everything around you starts to shake. For me, three values consistently guide how I (try to) lead:

- **Empathy**

- Integrity
- **A relentless focus on students**

Empathy isn't fluff—it's fuel.

Empathy isn't a weakness. And it's not soft.
It's strategic, transformative, and the fuel that powers connection, resilience, and belonging.

Empathy means leaning in when it would be easier to look away.
It's the decision to see—to see students, staff, and families not as data points or job titles but as human beings with stories.

I'll never forget the year we organized a holiday meal drive for needy families. It wasn't flashy, and it wasn't on the district calendar. It was heart work. Watching parents hold back tears as they loaded up food they couldn't afford... I'll never forget their gratitude or their relief.

That moment reminded me that leadership is service.
It's not just about goals and growth charts.
It's about showing up—especially when it matters most—and making people feel seen.

Integrity happens when no one is watching.

Integrity isn't about perfection. It's about alignment.

It's asking yourself daily:
Do my actions reflect my words?
Do my decisions echo my values?

Integrity lives in the quiet choices—the ones no one sees. And sometimes, especially in leadership, it lives in the moments when everyone's watching, and you still choose the harder right over the easier wrong.

I think of leaders like Abraham Lincoln, who faced impossible choices during one of the most divided moments in our nation's history. He didn't choose convenience—he chose conviction. He led with alignment, not approval.

Leadership today presents those same micro-moments of pressure. Moments where compromise whispers, "It would be easier if..." But when your compass is set to integrity, the direction stays clear— even when the road doesn't.

Student-Centered Leadership is my non-negotiable.
Every decision.
Every schedule tweak.
Every difficult conversation.
It all runs through one filter:
Is this what's best for kids?

Student-centered leadership isn't always the easiest path—but it's always the right one.

Sometimes, it means having hard conversations with adults. Sometimes, it means letting go of outdated traditions. Sometimes, it means saying no—when yes would make your life easier.

But your direction becomes clear when your North Star is student success—real, holistic, whole-child success, even when the journey isn't.

I've learned that student-first doesn't mean adult-last.
It means we lead with a lens of equity, courage, and care.
It means we do the right thing, even when it's uncomfortable.

Because students don't just need intense instruction—they need strong advocates.

And when the decision gets tough, the question remains simple: *Is this best for students?*

If the answer is yes, then the choice is already made.

When the Wind Blows, You'll Find Your Roots

Leadership will test you in ways you never expected.

You'll face moments when the ground shifts—when plans unravel, emotions run high, and everything feels fragile. In those moments, it's not your title or training that carries you. It's your values.

They're your roots.

And when the winds of pressure, urgency, or criticism blow, those roots will either hold or reveal how shallow they are.

It's easy to say you value empathy, integrity, or putting students first. But values are only proven when they're hard to live out.

When you're tired, dismissing the conversation would be easier—do you still lead with empathy?

When people are watching, and the pressure is on—do your actions still match your words?

When the easier decision serves adults, but the right decision serves kids—what do you choose?

That's where leadership gets real.
Not in the comfortable moments but in the costly ones.

And that's when you discover if your values are just aspirations—or actual anchors.

Daily Alignment Check: Am I Living What I Believe?

Defining your values is one thing.
Living them—especially under pressure—is something else entirely.

So, I started a habit: a simple daily self-check.

- Did my actions reflect what I say I believe?
- Where did I stay aligned?
- Where did I drift—and why?

Some days, the gap between what I value and how I lead is wide. But that's not failure—it's feedback. A chance to recalibrate and lead better tomorrow.

Turn Misalignment into Action

When your values and your behavior don't match, don't shame yourself—lead yourself.

If you value empathy but realize you've been short with your team, ask what needs to shift. More margin in your day? A pause before reacting? A "Tell me more" instead of a quick solution?

If you value integrity but find yourself overpromising, maybe it's time to say "no" more often—and mean it.

Minor course corrections add up.
Alignment lives in the repeatable moments, not the grand gestures.

Build in Accountability

Even the most grounded leaders drift without guardrails. Build in accountability:

- A mentor who calls it out.
- A sticky note reminder on your desk.
- A journal. A monthly team reflection.

Want to go deeper? Ask your staff:
Based on my behavior, what would you say my top three leadership values are?

If the answers don't match what you'd hope—good. That's insight. Use it.

Values in the Fire

One year, a district directive landed on my desk: remove students from intervention blocks due to behavior issues.

It felt wrong. These students needed support the most—and we were being asked to sideline them.

I could've complied quietly. But that silence would have spoken volumes. So I asked for a meeting and came prepared—with stories, data, and a calm but firm voice.

I didn't argue. I advocated. And to my surprise—they listened. We found a way forward that upheld both the policy and our values.

That moment reminded me:

- Values aren't just things you say. They're decisions in motion.
- Sometimes leadership sounds like, "Not here. Not like this."

Where Leadership is Defined

Leadership isn't defined in conference rooms but in the daily, pressure-filled moments.

- When a teacher's at their breaking point—do you lean in or look away?
- When a parent lashes out—do you react with defensiveness or respond with calm?
- When compliance contradicts conviction—do you go along or speak up?

These aren't hypotheticals. They're the daily realities where your values either hold... or fold.

Mirror Moment: Are You Leading What You Believe?

Ask yourself:

- If someone shadowed me for a week, what would they say I value?
- Where am I living what I say matters—and where am I drifting?
- Am I choosing comfort—or conviction?

This isn't about guilt. It's about clarity.
The best leaders don't get it perfect. They just get real.
They notice. They realign. They begin again.

You can't lead others well if you're not first grounded in who you are.

Practical Strategy: Create a Values Alignment Tracker

Each day for a week, take five minutes and jot this down:
- One leadership decision I made:
- Which value(s) did this reflect?
- Where did I feel off—and why?
- What small shift can I make tomorrow?

You'll start to see patterns.
You'll notice when empathy gives way to efficiency.
When people-pleasing hijacks your boundaries.
When student-first gets buried beneath adult comfort.

This is where authentic leadership lives:
In the tiny, honest course corrections that build trust, shape culture, and leave a legacy.

Know Who You Are: Leading with Core Values

Values can't just live on posters or in PD binders. They have to live in you.

Because when the stress hits, the ground shakes, and everything feels off...
You won't find your anchor in a flowchart.
You'll find it in your beliefs.

So, define what matters. Name it. Live it. Return to it often.
And when things get hard—don't run from your values. Run to them.

That's what defines your leadership.
Not the title. Not the test scores.

The alignment.

And when the next storm hits—you'll know where to begin again.

Leadership Soundtrack: When Conviction Meets Capacity

Track 3: "You Say" – Lauren Daigle

"You say I am strong when I think I am weak…"

Conviction gives us clarity. But even the clearest values can't keep us from breaking.

Every leader will face moments when their strength runs out.
When exhaustion blurs their identity.
When their convictions feel heavy to carry alone.

And still—the work continues.

The next chapter steps into that space:
The unraveling. The fall. And the quiet courage it takes to begin again.

Because it's one thing to lead with values.
It's another to lead through vulnerability.

And sometimes, the bravest thing you can do… is pause.

CHAPTER 4

From Breaking Point to Breakthrough

"SOMETHINGS YOU FALL WHEN YOU LEAD FROM THE EDGE. BUT FALLING ISN'T FAILING- IT PROVES YOU WERE BRAVE ENOUGH TO SHOW UP."

The Breaking Point

Some of the hardest lessons in leadership don't come with warning signs. They show up quietly—wrapped in exhaustion, layered in grief, and buried inside impossible decisions.

I didn't realize I was leading on empty until I started to crack.

We were still recovering from the tornado—relocated, patching things with duct tape and prayer. We were short-staffed, stretched thin, and holding space for students carrying more than their little hearts should.

Then, another year, here came the mold.
A summer HVAC failure meant more damage, disruption, and rebuilding. When I was told we had to empty out the classrooms again—for safety—the pushback hit hard.

I remember sitting in my car, sobbing into the steering wheel, too empty to drive home.
My leadership felt invisible.
My heart felt used up.

That day, strength didn't look like courage.
It looked like coming back the next day anyway.

And then, in yet another year, we lost her.
Our school counselor.
The soul of our building.
The steady hand, the quiet check-in, the hallway laugh.

Her coffee cup was still on her desk.
Her pictures were still on her wall.

And my body finally said: *enough.*

My hand was cramping when I tried to write or use the computer.
My heart raced through simple tasks. I couldn't eat. Couldn't sleep.
Couldn't cry. It felt like walking underwater.

This was the fall.

The Real Meaning of Resilience

I used to think resilience meant bouncing back fast.
Now I know it means rebuilding—honestly, slowly, and fully.

It doesn't look like power poses.
It looks like journaling with trembling hands.
Praying through numbness.
Saying, "I'm not okay," and still trying.

Eventually, I made the appointment.

I sat in a counselor's office—no title, no to-do list—just a human.
And for the first time in months, I exhaled.

Resilience doesn't erase the fall.
It simply gives you the courage to rise again—soul-tired but willing.

Naming the Season, Holding the Mirror

I stopped pretending.
I let myself feel it all—and reflect honestly.

Mirror Moment: Grows and Glows

At the end of each day, I asked:
- What went well?
- What challenged me?
- What do I want to do differently tomorrow?

Some days, the only answer was: I showed up. And that was enough.

The reflection tool I had created for my staff?
It quietly saved me.
Because I wasn't evaluating—I was remembering who I was underneath the burnout.

Regulating the Fall: The Window and the Line

Dysregulation starts to feel normal when you stay in survival mode too long.

Heather Forbes' Window of Tolerance gave me a language for what was happening—to me, my team, and our students.

Sometimes we were hyperaroused—anxious, reactive, overstimulated.
Sometimes, we shut down—silent, numb, detached.

We began to name it.

"I think I'm outside my window right now."

And instead of shame—we met it with compassion.

Alongside that, we began using the Above and Below the Line language:
- Above the Line: engaged, honest, accountable.
- Below the Line: defensive, blaming, disengaged.

It wasn't about labeling people.

It was about offering grace.

We'd ask:
What would help you get back above?
Do you want me to sit with you or give you space? It changed everything.

Let Them—Then Lead

There were days I carried every complaint, eye-roll, and sideways comment like bricks in a backpack.

Until I found the "Let Them" Theory.

Let them question. Let them resist. Let them gossip.

You don't have to fix it.
You just have to stay grounded.

"Let them" wasn't a weakness.

It was wisdom.
It was sanity-saving.
It was strength disguised as stillness.

And then—I led anyway.

 ## Mirror Moment: Above or Below the Line

Ask yourself:
- Where have I been operating lately?
- What throws me below the line?
- What brings me back?

The more self-aware you are, the safer others feel around you.

Strong Cultures Outlast Tough Seasons

We couldn't fake strength—so we built safety instead.

We checked in.
We brought meals.
We left sticky notes.
We dressed in ridiculous costumes, played Bunco, and gathered for "Coffee & Chit Chat."

When someone spiraled—we didn't fix it.
We sat beside them.

Joy wasn't a luxury.
It was our strategy.
It was survival.

Because you don't build a culture with initiatives.
You build it with humans who feel seen.

That's how you survive a tornado and still sing Christmas carols in December. That's how you lose someone sacred and still laugh again. That's how resilience becomes *collective*.

Practical Strategy: Leading Your Own Reset Retreat

I knew I couldn't keep leading on fumes. So, I created my own kind of reset.

Try this the next time you're running on empty:
- Create Space: Block 90 quiet minutes away from your school building.
- Reflect Honestly: What's working? What's not? What hurts?
- Set One Reset Intention: You'll protect, change, or release one thing in the next 30 days.
- Tell One Person: Share it. Let them check in with you.

You don't have to retreat to reset. You just need room to reconnect.

FALLING ISN'T FAILING—IT PROVES YOU WERE BRAVE ENOUGH TO SHOW UP.

Falling Isn't Failing

There are days you'll feel like quitting. There are days you'll cry in your car. There are days your hand will cramp from stress, and your mind will scream, I can't do this anymore.

And still—you will rise.

You'll rise gentler.
You'll rise wiser.
You'll rise more human.

You'll remember that leadership isn't about being perfect. It's about being present. And some days, that presence will change everything.

Leadership Soundtrack: From Burnout to Boundaries

Track 4: "Fight Song" – Rachel Platten

"This is my fight song / Take back my life song..."

After the fall comes the reckoning—not with others, but with yourself. When the noise fades and the grief quiets, you're left with the most powerful question a leader can ask:

How do I lead myself back to life?

The next chapter moves inward—into rhythms, boundaries, and habits that restore more than just energy—they rebuild your soul. Because the strongest leaders aren't the ones who never break. They're the ones who know when to stop, reset, and rise differently.

And that's where real leadership begins again.

CHAPTER 5

Leading Yourself First- The Power of Self- Leadership and Recommitment

"You can't lead others where you haven't led yourself."

Somewhere between surviving and thriving, there's a choice. It doesn't come with fireworks or applause. It usually comes quietly, maybe while sitting in a parked car after a long day, wondering if it's all worth it. It's when you realize the rebuild isn't just about your school—it's about you.

We talk a lot about serving others—about showing up for our students, our staff, and our families. But how often do we talk about what it means to show up for ourselves? Not with perfection, not with presence, not with clarity, not with intention.

The truth is that superheroes don't lead the greatest schools. They're led by human beings—who have learned to lead themselves first.

The Shift

After the fall, things change not all at once. But little by little, clarity creeps in.

You begin to see your schedule not as a badge of honor but as a boundary. You notice when your energy dips—and give yourself permission to step back. You don't say yes to everything. You don't run on fumes anymore. You start to protect your peace like it's part of the school improvement plan—because it is.

This shift is the quiet beginning of self-leadership.

The Day I Led Myself Differently

There was a Monday when everything went wrong. Staff was tense, a parent yelled in the office, and the copier was out of toner—again. In the past, I would've absorbed it all and smiled through it. Tried to fix everything. Pushed through with clenched teeth and a racing mind.

But that day, something clicked.

I walked to the staff lounge, filled my coffee, and instead of diving back into the chaos, I took 90 seconds—just 90. I stood there, breathing slowly, not fixing, not solving, just being.

Then I walked back into the storm and didn't carry it like I used to. I led it instead.

That was the moment I realized leadership isn't about doing more. It's about being clear about who you are and how you show up. It's about leading yourself on purpose, not on autopilot.

The Rebuild of Principal Salinas

Take Principal Julia Salinas.

After a devastating flood destroyed much of her South Texas school, she spent the first month sleeping on a cot in the gym, helping families get food and basic supplies. Her entire community was watching her—and she was running on empty.

> **LEADERSHIP ISN'T ABOUT DOING MORE. IT'S ABOUT BEING CLEAR ABOUT WHO YOU ARE AND HOW YOU SHOW UP.**

"I was showing up for everyone but myself," she told me. "I kept thinking, 'I just need to get us through this.' But I didn't realize how I got us through it mattered more than I thought."

She finally took a day off, then a weekend. She started walking in the mornings, journaling again, and intentionally involving her leadership team in decision-making. She stopped wearing exhaustion like a badge. And when she returned, she wasn't just a stronger leader—she was a more grounded one.

"When I led myself well, everything else got better," she said. "The team, the energy, even the way we made decisions. It wasn't about me being stronger. It was about me being centered."

Mirror Moments (Revisited)

We introduced Mirror Moments in earlier chapters as a time to get brutally honest with yourself. But here, they shift.

Now your Mirror Moment isn't "What broke me?" It becomes:
- What centers me?
- Where am I giving too much away?
- What habits bring me peace, not pressure?
- What does my team feel when I walk into the room?
- Am I leading from clarity or chaos?

Leading yourself first means building in rhythms of reflection before the crisis forces you to.

The Practices of Self-Leadership

Self-leadership doesn't mean being perfect. It means being present—with yourself and your purpose. Here are a few practical tools to anchor your own leadership rhythm:

The Morning Re-Center
- A 5-minute check-in before the day begins.
- Ask yourself: What's one thing I will control today? What's one thing I can release?
- Speak gratitude. Name your intention. Then go.

Friday 15
- Take 15 minutes on Friday to reflect.
- What were your glows and grows this week?
- Did you lead like the person you want to be?

The Clarity Check
- Once a month, revisit your "why."
- Are you still leading in alignment with it?
- If not—adjust. No guilt. Just recalibrate.

The Self-Check Template
A 1-page monthly tracker to include the following: Energy levels, Wins to celebrate, Boundary check, Leadership joy moments, What needs to shift

Leadership is Contagious—So is Burnout

When you lead yourself well, your team sees it. They learn that it's okay to set boundaries, to be reflective, and to show up with authenticity instead of adrenaline.

Self-leadership is not selfish. It's *strategic*.

It's how we model sustainability.
It's how we avoid becoming cautionary tales.
It's how we shift from survival...to significance.

Leadership Soundtrack: From Survival to Systems

Track 5: "Rise Up" – Andra Day

"And I'll rise up / I'll rise like the day..." A crisis may shake the ground beneath us, but culture—when built on purpose—holds. And when leaders shift from reaction to intention, something powerful happens: resilience becomes embedded, not improvised. As we move into the next chapter, we expand beyond the school walls and into the rhythms, systems, and supports that sustain us. Because rising isn't just about this moment—it's about building something strong enough to keep rising repeatedly. And that's what we're doing now.

Part 2:

Culture That Sticks

CHAPTER 6

Culture Over Crisis- What Lasts When Everything Else Changes

"IN TIMES OF CRISIS, WE DON'T RISE TO THE LEVEL OF OUR GOALS- WE FALL TO THE LEVEL OF OUR SYSTEMS." JAMES CLEAR.

What Outlasts the Storm

Education has always come in waves—but this season felt relentless.

We barely had time to catch our breath before the next crisis arrived. After finally stepping into our newly rebuilt building in 2019, the pandemic hit. Masks. Protocols. Uncertainty. Loss.

And then, in August of 2022, we lost my school counselor—my friend, my co-leader, my anchor. COVID took her from us, and it hit me harder than I could have imagined.

I missed her.

I needed her.
I grieved her.
And I battled the guilt of grieving when others needed me to be strong.

I had no assistant principal. Now, no counselor. The weight of leadership grew heavy—heavier than I could carry alone.

I couldn't even open her office door.

There was no training, strategy, or checklist to fix what we were walking through. Resilience didn't feel like a rallying cry—it felt like just trying to breathe through the day. And still, no matter how much I gave, it never felt like enough.

So I asked myself a question: *What, within my control, will outlast the circumstances?*

The answer wasn't a plan. It wasn't a policy.
It was **culture**.

Leadership is Not About Reaction—It's About Intentionality

Authentic leadership isn't about reacting to the crisis in front of you. It's about building something that can withstand whatever comes next.

The truth is obstacles in school leadership aren't optional. Some shake the foundation. Others wear you down slowly. But either way—they come.

What separates schools that survive from those that thrive isn't funding, innovation, or a perfect plan. It's culture—a culture built on purpose, strengthened over time, and upheld by shared values.

When the tornado destroyed our school, we thought replacing supplies and rebuilding classrooms was the most challenging part. We assumed that we'd be okay once students had desks and teachers had resources.

We were wrong.

The real work wasn't about walls or whiteboards.
It was about restoring belonging.
Helping staff and students feel safe again. Seen again. Held again.

Then came more loss. The death of our counselor shook the foundation once more. And this time, I wasn't just holding space for others—I was carrying my own grief, too.

It would've been easy to stay in survival mode. And for a while, I did. I reacted. I managed. I moved from one fire to the next.

If you had asked me then, I would have told you, "I'm doing my best." And I was. But now I see it more clearly—survival mode isn't sustainable leadership.

Crisis management might get you through the week.
But only culture will carry you through the year.

CRISIS MANAGEMENT MIGHT GET YOU THROUGH THE WEEK. BUT ONLY CULTURE WILL CARRY YOU THROUGH THE YEAR.

And for a while, I lost sight of that. I let the chaos steer me. Until I remembered—our strength wasn't in what we had lost.

It was in what we had *built*.

Understanding the Window of Tolerance: A Game-Changer for School Culture

One of the most transformational tools we discovered during our hardest seasons was the Window of Tolerance, a framework developed by Dr. Dan Siegel and expanded by Heather Forbes in *Help for Billy* (2012).

This concept became a lifeline.

The Window of Tolerance describes the optimal emotional state in which a person can think clearly, learn effectively, and respond to stress with balance. When we stay within that window, we can function.

But when stress overwhelms us?

We fall outside it.

- **Hyperarousal** looks like fight or flight: anxiety, anger, reactivity.
- **Hypoarousal** looks like freeze or shutdown: withdrawal, numbness, disengagement.

And it's not just students. Teachers fall outside their window. Leaders do, too.

During our hardest years—post-tornado, during the pandemic, after our counselor's death—we were all outside our window. Often. Sometimes without even realizing it.

We were operating in survival mode and calling it leadership.

That realization changed everything.

How Learning About the Window of Tolerance Changed Our Approach

Once I understood the Window of Tolerance, it reframed a lot about how I approached things.

What we were dealing with wasn't just exhaustion—it was dysregulation on a massive scale.

We expected teachers to manage intense behaviors and trauma without understanding the neurological barriers students were facing. And we weren't acknowledging that we, the adults, were dysregulated too.

Here's how it works:
- Hyperarousal occurs when someone is pushed above their window. They may become anxious, panicked, irritable, or aggressive. Their nervous system is in overdrive—on edge and highly reactive.

- Hypoarousal occurs when someone drops below their window. They might shut down, dissociate, zone out, or feel numb. It's not defiance—it's the body conserving energy, trying to disappear.

This applies to students. To teachers. To all of us.

When I introduced this concept to my team, it was like a lightbulb turned on. Suddenly, the behaviors that had felt frustrating or overwhelming made sense.

Instead of labeling a student as "defiant" or "checked out," we started asking:
- *Is this student outside their window?*
- *Are they stuck in fight, flight, or freeze?*
- *What can we do to help them regulate and return to learning?*

This was the shift—from reaction to response.
Everything felt different once we had language for what we were living through.

Implementing This Learning in Our School Culture

That awareness became our foundation for healing and rebuilding.

We realized that dysregulation wasn't just a student issue but an everyone issue.

Our teachers were depleted. Their emotional capacity had shrunk, and their ability to respond with patience and empathy was worn thin. So we flipped the script: We stopped focusing solely on student behavior and started with staff regulation first.

We taught breathing techniques, built in movement breaks, and modeled mindfulness strategies. We embedded calming tools into our staff meetings and trainings—not just for students but also for the adults who were holding everyone else up.

The result?
Teachers felt seen.
They realized they didn't have to "push through" or pretend.
They had permission to care for themselves first—so they could care better for others.

We weren't just handing them tools.
We were giving them back capacity.

It restored what burnout had taken—capacity, clarity, and care.

Creating Trauma-Informed Responses to Behavior

As we continued learning, we stopped asking,
"What's wrong with this student?"
and started asking,
"What does this student need right now to return to regulation?"

That shift in mindset reshaped our entire discipline approach.

We began by creating safe spaces in classrooms—quiet corners with sensory tools, fidgets, breathing prompts, and calming visuals. These are not time-out zones, not punishment zones, but spaces to come back into balance.

We gave students tools, not just rules.

We also re-trained how we responded in moments of disruption. Instead of escalating with authority, we leaned in with curiosity:

- What might have triggered this?
- Where are they in their Window of Tolerance?

- How can I co-regulate instead of control?

We also changed our language. Instead of labels like "defiant" or "lazy," we helped students name their emotions. We taught them that self-regulation is a skill, not a fixed trait—something you can learn, practice, and strengthen.

The impact?
Students began to feel seen.
Behaviors shifted.
Teachers felt less powerless and more purposeful.

Discipline stopped feeling like a battle—and started looking more like coaching. More like care.

Embedding Regulation into Leadership

One of the most important truths I've learned is this: **Leaders are not immune to dysregulation.**

We carry stress.
We carry grief.
We carry guilt.
And often, we carry it quietly.

In the months after losing our school counselor, I stayed in motion. I overextended, micromanaged, and buried myself in tasks. I isolated myself emotionally. I convinced myself I was fine because people needed me to be.

But I wasn't leading from a grounded place.
I was leading from survival.

The turning point came when I started recognizing my own patterns. I could feel it when I crossed my threshold—reacting instead of responding, controlling instead of connecting.

That awareness didn't come from a workshop. It came from hard conversations, honest reflection, and counseling. Therapy became my lifeline. Sitting across from someone who didn't need me to be "on," who asked nothing of me except to be real, was freeing, healing, and clarifying.

Now, I recommend it without hesitation—not as a weakness but a leadership strength.

Because the truth is, if you don't learn to regulate yourself, your dysregulation becomes part of the system. And no strategy or system can compensate for a leader running on empty.

The Oxygen Mask & God's Big Signs

You've heard the airplane safety reminder:
"Put your oxygen mask on first before helping others."

Sounds simple. Logical. Smart.

But for a long time, here's what I believed: *If I just make sure everyone else has theirs, surely there'll be enough air left for me, too.*

Spoiler alert: that's not how it works.

I've learned—sometimes the hard way—that clarity fades when I skip my care. My patience thins. My leadership suffers.

And just when I convince myself I'm fine, that I'm managing— God tends to send a flashing neon sign.

A tornado.

Half of my body going numb.

Or a moment so ridiculous I can't help but laugh... then cry.

He knows I'm a slow learner. So He goes big. But I'm learning.
Slowly.

To pause.

To breathe.

To take the walk.

Drink the water.

Pray.

Text a friend.

Put the mask on.

Because leading through chaos requires fuel.

And sometimes, that fuel is spiritual.

Sometimes physical.

And sometimes... it's a Diet Dr. Pepper and five minutes of silence in the school parking lot.

Whatever it is—**it matters.**

The Lasting Impact: A Culture That Grows Through Challenge

Once our staff began to understand their own patterns—what pushed them into overdrive or shutdown—we were able to build a different kind of culture.

Not one that ignored stress. One that acknowledged it. Not one that pushed through pain. One that learned how to pause, regulate, and recover.

We changed the tone of our classrooms, strengthened our teams, and even improved staff retention—not because things got easier but because people felt equipped, supported, and part of the team.

We stopped reacting. We started asking better questions.

We created space for hard conversations. We built systems for check-ins, not just checklists.

We normalized being human. We permitted ourselves and others to say, "I'm not okay," without judgment. And we taught ourselves—and each other—how to come back to center.

The storms didn't stop. But we learned to anchor deeper.

The truth is that you can't control every crisis, but you can build a culture that outlasts it.

The Importance of Consistency and Shared Values

If you want to build a lasting culture, you need Consistency and shared values.

Consistency Builds Trust

Your actions must match your words.
The trust breaks if a leader talks about collaboration but makes decisions in isolation.

Consistency isn't about perfection. It's about integrity over time.

One year, I adopted a guiding question I often shared with staff: **"Is this what's best for kids?"**

That simple filter became our foundation. We used it in budget meetings, discipline decisions, and hallway conversations. If something didn't align, we paused, reconsidered, and adjusted.

The more consistently I reinforced that value, the more others started doing it. It became our filter—not just mine.

Culture isn't built in assemblies or slogans.
It's built in how you show up—every day, especially when it's hard.

Shared Values Create Unity

Policies don't hold a school together—shared purpose does.

In one school, our leadership team collaborated with staff to name five core values: **Respect. Collaboration. Growth. Kindness. Accountability.**

They weren't just posters on the wall.
They were the lens we used to coach, support, and celebrate one another. They shaped how we spoke, how we solved problems, and how we stayed grounded when things got messy.

When everyone knows what we stand for, we waste less energy figuring out how to respond. We come back to the values—not the volume of the moment.

Shared values don't just keep things running. They keep people connected—even in chaos.

Leading with Intention, Not Reaction

A thriving culture isn't built in response to crisis—it's built **before** it.

It holds the school together when everything else feels like it's falling apart. It's the deep belief that our purpose is bigger than our problems, that our values aren't just nice words—they're our North Star.

And if I've learned anything, it's this: **Culture is a choice—and it's never "done."**

You either shape it, or it shapes you.

You either lead with intention, or you react from exhaustion.

In the hardest seasons, your systems don't save you.
Your strategies don't carry you.
Your culture does.

It's the thread that weaves through the chaos.
The reason people stay.
The reason students feel safe enough to try again.

So, ask yourself:
- Are you leading from intention or impulse?
- Are you shaping the culture, or is it shaping you?
- Are your decisions rooted in values—or reactions?

Because leadership isn't just about getting through today. It's about building something that still stands tomorrow.

Mirror Moment: Are You Leading Intentionally—or Reactively?

Pause and reflect: Do you respond with clarity or react from fear or urgency in times of uncertainty?

Ask yourself:

- What parts of my leadership feel grounded and aligned with my values?
- Where do I catch myself operating in "crisis mode," putting out fires instead of building fireproof systems?
- What's one shift I can make to lead more proactively tomorrow?

Leadership isn't about avoiding challenges but choosing how you'll lead through it.

What intentional actions can you take today to strengthen your school's foundation for the future?

Practical Strategy: Five Ways to Lead with Intention, Not Reaction

1. **Anchor Every Decision in Core Values** - Before moving forward, pause and ask: Does this align with what we believe? Staying values-centered keeps your leadership steady—even when everything else feels uncertain.

2. **Shift from Crisis Response to Crisis Preparedness** - Instead of waiting for challenges to arise, create proactive systems that support both staff and students. This includes implementing staff wellness plans, establishing strong student support strategies, and offering ongoing professional development that anticipates needs rather than merely responding to them.
   a. Staff wellness plans
   b. Student support strategies
   c. Ongoing PD that anticipates—not just responds to—challenges

3. **Create Psychological Safety** - Make it safe for your staff to speak up, innovate, and ask for help. When people feel safe, they lead and collaborate with more courage.

4. **Reinforce Stability Through Structure** - In chaos, people crave consistency. Clear expectations, shared routines, and predictable rhythms calm the storm.

5. **Model What You Expect** — How you handle small, everyday moments will shape how your team responds to big ones. Stay rooted. Communicate clearly. Choose presence over panic.

Intentional leadership isn't about controlling every moment. It's about creating the conditions for people to thrive through any moment.

Leading with Resilience and Intention

The storms will come.
Sometimes, one at a time.
Sometimes, all at once.

Crisis is inevitable—but chaos doesn't have to be. The schools that thrive aren't those with flawless systems, but those grounded in strong, intentional culture. When a school is rooted in purpose, strengthened by consistency, and sustained by shared values, it can weather any storm with resilience and clarity.

Learning about the Window of Tolerance gave us more than a new language—it gave us a way forward. We moved from surviving to stabilizing, from burnout to balance, from fear to faith in something lasting.

To lead with intention is to choose clarity over chaos. Connection over control. Purpose over panic. True leadership isn't about standing on steady ground. It's about showing up on the frontlines of change—ready to rise, and help others rise, too.

Leadership Soundtrack: From Isolation to Impact

Track 6: "Brighter Days" – Blessing Offor

"I know there's gonna be some brighter days / I swear that love will find you in your pain..."

Culture shifts when people stop surviving and start showing up for each other. It's not about a program—it's about people. When collaboration replaces isolation and connection replaces control, everything changes.

In the next chapter, we don't just lead—we build.
We invest.
We rise—**together.**
Because brighter days don't just appear.
They are built.
By leaders who believe.

CHAPTER 7

Transforming School Culture- The Shift That Changed Everything

"CULTURE EATS STRATEGY FOR BREAKFAST."- PETER DRUCKER

A Culture of Survival vs. A Culture of Collaboration

Today, when you walk into our school, the energy is unmistakable.

There's movement. Connection. Momentum.

Teachers gather in small groups—not because they have to, but because they want to. Students walk the halls with confidence, knowing they're seen, supported, and cared for. Learning thrives not just because of strong instructional practices but also because of a culture that refuses to let anyone fall through the cracks.

But it wasn't always this way.

A few years ago, the school felt heavy—not because people didn't care—but because they were tired, disconnected, and in survival mode.

On one of my first days, a veteran teacher said quietly, "I love my kids... but I'm tired. I just don't know if what I do here really matters. We're just 'X' Elementary."

That moment stuck with me.

But what broke something open in me came later that same week. I walked into the teacher's lounge during lunch on a Monday. It was silent. There was no conversation, no laughter, just isolation. Teachers sat alone in classrooms—grading, answering emails, eating at their desks.

It wasn't coldness. It was fatigue.

They had been doing it alone for so long they didn't know how to do it together.

That's when I realized: The biggest challenge ahead wasn't academic. It was relational.

We couldn't talk about test scores or PLCs until we rebuilt trust. We had to shift from isolation to collaboration, from compliance to commitment, from "my classroom" to "our school."

THE BIGGEST CHALLENGE AHEAD WASN'T ACADEMIC. IT WAS RELATIONAL.

And that shift wouldn't come from a memo.
It had to be lived—one relationship, conversation, and decision at a time.

Building a Foundation for Cultural Change

To change a culture, you don't start with policies—you start with people.

I began by listening—not leading with a checklist but with conversations—intentional, agenda-free conversations with the people who had been there, showing up through the hard seasons.

I asked:

- What do you love about teaching here?
- What frustrates you the most?
- What would it be if you could change one thing about our culture?
- What do you need from me to feel supported?

Those conversations uncovered two essential truths:

- Our teachers deeply cared about their students.
- But they didn't feel connected to each other—or to a shared purpose.

Their frustration wasn't resistance to change. It was fatigue from constant change that felt disconnected from their voices.

That's when I knew: If we wanted real transformation, it couldn't come from the top. It had to come from **within.**

So I looked for the culture carriers—the informal leaders whose words carried weight in the lounge, whose quiet influence shaped how others showed up. They didn't all have titles, but they had trust, and that made them the cornerstone of what we'd build next.

Creating a Unified Purpose - From Compliance to Commitment

You can't transform culture through top-down mandates. You transform it through a shared vision and deep ownership.

So we started asking big questions—together:

- What do we want our school to stand for?
- What do we believe about student success?
- What are the non-negotiables in every classroom?
- How do we want to treat each other, even when it's hard?

These weren't meetings. They were moments of clarity, honesty, and connection. Out of those conversations came something powerful: our Mutual Expectations Document.

Not a checklist. Not a contract. A declaration of shared purpose.

We defined what collaboration looked like. We clarified how we communicate—with families and with each other. We agreed on how we support students, plan instruction, and build relationships.

It wasn't compliance—it was commitment. This document wasn't handed down—it was built together. It wasn't about policies—it was about identity—who we were choosing to become as a school.

However, a shared vision only matters if it moves beyond paper. If it stays on a poster, it's just decoration. So we got to work, making sure that what we believed actually shaped how we showed up every day.

Building Buy-In and Trust

Once our purpose was clear, the next step was building something harder: buy-in. Actual culture change doesn't happen because the principal says it will. It happens when every educator feels seen, heard, and genuinely invested in the work.

So, we focused on three essential pillars:

1. **Purposeful Visioning:** We didn't create a vision just to check a box—we made sure it meant something. Every goal, initiative, and system had to reflect our shared beliefs.

2. **Empowered Leadership at Every Level:** We invited teachers to lead the changes they cared most about. They weren't just expected to implement the vision—they were part of shaping it.

3. **Consistency + Follow-Through:** Trust grew slowly through every decision, every check-in, every time we did what we said we'd do. That consistency became the quiet drumbeat of cultural change.

And yes, it wasn't easy. Some staff struggled with the shift, and a few eventually chose to leave.

That was hard. But it was also necessary.

Because if we were going to build something real, we needed a team that was aligned not just in skill but also in belief.

And those who stayed? They became the foundation of something powerful: a school no longer driven by survival but by shared responsibility and collective growth.

Building Trust Through Consistency and Follow-through

One of the greatest threats to school culture is not resistance—it's distrust. Teachers have lived through top-down mandates before. They've seen shiny new initiatives fade. If this shift was going to last, it couldn't ride on energy alone. It had to be built on credibility.

So, we anchored every decision in transparency and purpose.

If we introduced a new initiative, we started with the why. If something didn't align with our mission, we questioned it—together.

We took small, strategic steps.
We focused on quick wins before big changes.
We piloted learning walks.
We refined how teams used collaboration time.
We built consistency around using data to drive instruction.

And then—we celebrated.

Every new strategy tested.
Every teacher who took a risk.
Every student's success—no matter how small.

We didn't just celebrate to boost morale.
We celebrated to show *that this matters. We see you.*

We also made sure support wasn't just encouragement—it was equipping.

Through coaching, PLCs, and targeted PD, we gave teachers tools to grow—not just expectations to meet.

Trust wasn't built through big announcements. It was built through reliability. Through listening. Through showing up. Through honoring the work already happening—and helping take it even further.

From Small Wins to Lasting Change

Once the foundation was steady, the momentum started to build. We raised expectations—not just for students but for ourselves. PLCs became non-negotiable—not just a meeting but a mindset. Collaboration, data analysis, and shared problem-solving became part of how we operated daily—not because we had to, but because it worked.

And we celebrated *every step forward*:
- A new instructional strategy tried.
- A breakthrough with a tough student.
- A team that came together to analyze data and adjust a plan.

No win was too small to recognize—because small wins compound.

One of the most transformative shifts was implementing learning walks—peer-led classroom visits focused on growth, not evaluation. Teachers visited each other's classrooms, shared insights, and reflected together.

What began as a quarterly initiative quickly became a monthly norm—not because we mandated it, but because teachers saw the value of learning from each other in real-time.

Another turning point was introducing the Big 5 Data Initiative—a simplified way to track and discuss key data points. At first, there was hesitancy. But over time, data moved from something we feared to something that empowered us.

This opened the door to full standards-based instruction, which was a game-changer in how we planned, assessed, and supported student learning.

We stopped guessing.
We started responding.
And it showed.

What It Looks Like Now (And Why It Still Gives Me Chills)

The other day, I walked past the teacher's lounge—not because something was wrong, but because something was so right I had to stop and take it in.

There was laughter.

Teachers were swapping weekend stories, and someone passed around homemade brownies. There was no venting, no complaints, just connection.

They genuinely enjoyed being together.
I stood there quietly and thought,
This is it. This is what it's supposed to feel like.

This is what happens when people feel safe, seen, and supported.

That moment didn't come from a single program or PD session.
It came from a culture rebuilt—one decision, one conversation, one human at a time.

And every time I witness it, it still gives me chills.

The Reality of Change—Some Will Stay, Some Will Go

Change is hard. It stretches people. It stirs discomfort. And sometimes, it reveals what no longer fits. When we committed to transforming our school's culture, I knew not everyone would join us. Not because they didn't care but because they were used to doing things a certain way, and this shift required something different.

Some teachers had spent years working in silos, managing their classrooms as islands. They were dedicated. Hardworking. But collaboration, shared ownership, and transparency threatened the autonomy they'd always known.

Their resistance wasn't rooted in defiance. It was rooted in fear—fear that this would be just another initiative, fear of losing control, fear of change that might not last.

Some asked, "How do we know this isn't just another thing?" And I understood. We've all seen initiatives come and go. But this wasn't a program. This was about rewriting who we were as a school—and that doesn't happen overnight.

So, instead of pushing people forward, we made space for honest dialogue, listened, and responded with clarity and reassurance. Collaboration wasn't about losing independence; it was about multiplying impact.

Still, a few eventually chose to leave. That was painful, but it was necessary. Culture is defined not just by who stays but by what we are willing to release. We are only as good as the weakest behavior we will allow. That is BIG.

Letting go doesn't mean dishonoring the past. It means owning the future. It means saying with clarity: This is who we are. This is what we stand for. And this is where we're going.

And for those who stayed, that clarity became a source of strength. They didn't just know the expectations—they believed in them. New hires came in aligned from day one. And over time, we didn't just build a stronger team—we built a stronger identity.

Because real leadership means making hard choices, and the most defining moments don't come when things are easy. They come when you choose to lead forward anyway.

Sustaining the Shift—What Made the Changes Stick?

Years later, this school doesn't just feel different. It is different. It is no longer surviving; it's thriving.

Teachers don't close their doors and go it alone. They plan together, lean on each other, and problem-solve as a team.

Instruction is no longer driven by preference or tradition. It's rooted in real-time, meaningful data that drives decisions and helps teachers meet students exactly where they are.

PLCs aren't just scheduled. They're lived. They aren't a box to check. They're a mindset—a commitment to shared growth that shows up in every hallway conversation and team meeting.

Accountability doesn't flow top-down anymore. It's shared. Teachers hold each other to high standards, not out of pressure but of pride in the work and belief in the vision.

But the most important shift is this: the mindset. Teachers don't just see themselves as individuals doing their best. They see themselves as part of something bigger. They belong to a culture, a mission, a movement.

That mindset didn't just improve the culture—it sustained it.

The Work That Never Ends—Keeping Culture at the Forefront

As our culture evolved, so did our systems. This wasn't a one-time transformation. It became a way of operating. We built intentional structures around sustainability, shared leadership, and growth to keep the culture strong and forward-moving.

One of the most impactful was the formation of our Guiding Coalition—an application-based team of teacher leaders. These weren't symbolic positions. They were trusted voices. They sat at decision-making tables, helped shape building-wide priorities, and ensured that real-time classroom needs stayed front and center.

We also introduced annual summer retreats—not just PD days, but sacred time to reset and reconnect. We revisited our mission, vision, and commitments. We remembered our why.

Collaboration deepened, especially between general education and special education teams. Intentional team design helped ensure students got layered, inclusive support. It wasn't one program—it was a shared mindset: *Every learner matters.*

Our Every Student, Every Standard document was one of the most powerful tools to emerge. It allowed us to track each student's progress on essential standards at a glance, identifying who was mastering them, who needed intervention, and how we'd respond.

It didn't just measure learning; it shaped how we taught. It didn't just catch kids before they fell through the cracks; it helped us build bridges before they even reached the edge.

These systems didn't just support the culture; they protected it and kept it visible, living, and growing.

As James Clear says, *"You don't rise to the level of your goals. You fall to the level of your systems."* In schools, vision matters—but systems sustain it. Without consistent structures, culture slips. But with them, culture becomes what we hope for and how we operate every day.

Mirror Moment: Anything You Want to Improve?

Remember when you felt fully connected—part of something greater than yourself. What made that moment so meaningful?

Now, contrast it with a time you felt isolated or uncertain. What shifted?

Most schools exist somewhere in the tension between those two realities. But culture is not fixed—it moves and responds to what we model.

So ask yourself: If someone walked into your school today, what would they feel? Would they sense a culture of collaboration, shared purpose, and collective responsibility? Or would they notice survival, isolation, and disconnection?

Take a moment to reflect:

- What area of your school culture needs strengthening right now?
- How can teacher leaders be part of that solution?
- What's one small action you can take this week to move toward something better?

Culture doesn't change overnight. It shifts through intention—one conversation, one moment, one step at a time.

Practical Strategy: The Power of Glows and Grows—A Reflective Leadership Tool

One of the most impactful strategies we implemented was a simple but powerful process: Glows and Grows. It wasn't about evaluations or compliance. It was about creating space for open dialogue, mutual trust, and reflection that fuels real growth. I send all staff members a Glows and Grows feedback form each year. They reflect on:

Glows – What's going well? What are your strengths? Where do you feel confident and proud?
Grows – What's challenging? Where do you want to grow? How can leadership support you?

Then, I meet with every single staff member one-on-one. There is no rubric, no clipboard, just presence, curiosity, and care.

Yes, it takes time. But the return is trust, transparency, connection, and insight I would have missed otherwise.

I've had teachers share things they never told anyone—personal struggles, unspoken frustrations, hidden hopes. One conversation sparked a mentoring relationship that transformed a teacher's confidence—and mine.

Why Grows and Glows Work

It sends a clear message:
- Every educator has something worth celebrating.
- Every educator has areas where they want to grow—and that's not a weakness.
- Leadership is here to listen, not judge.

Because it's non-evaluative, it builds vulnerability and safety. It reminds people that they are more than a performance score. They are a person, and their voice matters.

How It Changed Our Culture

Before this process, many teachers felt disconnected. Some felt unseen. Others quietly carried the weight of challenges they didn't feel safe sharing. Glows and Grows changed that.

It shifted the tone of our building—from silent suffering to shared reflection, from fear to feedback, from compliance to connection.

Teachers started mirroring this approach with students, naming strengths, building goals, and celebrating growth. It became part of who we were.

How To Start

1. **Use a Simple Feedback Form:** A Google Form works. Keep questions open-ended and reflective.
2. **Schedule One-on-One Conversations:** Protect the time. Listen more than you speak. Be fully present.
3. **Act on What You Learn:** If a theme emerges—act on it. If a win is shared—amplify it.
4. **Repeat and Reinforce:** This isn't a one-time event. Make it a habit. Let it shape how you coach, lead, and respond.

Leadership that Listens

Culture doesn't grow from mandates.
It grows from trust.
From presence.
From a leader who makes time to listen, even when everything feels busy.

Glows and Grows may seem simple. But in practice, it becomes the heartbeat of a school that puts people first.

And that's where real change always begins.

Leadership Soundtrack: From Gratitude to Grace

Track 7: "Kind and Generous" – Natalie Merchant

"I want to thank you / Thank you / For your kindness..."

Gratitude keeps us soft in a complicated world. But it doesn't stop with a thank you—it shows up in how we lead, respond, and hold space for people... even on their hardest days.

The next chapter takes us deeper—into the kind of love that's not vague or fluffy but bold and transformational. In leadership, love isn't just a feeling. It's a decision we repeatedly make to show up with compassion, courage, and unwavering belief in the people we serve.

And that kind of love?

It doesn't just shape culture. It shapes lives.

Gratitude as the Fuel for Connection

If You Want to Change a School, Change What You Look For

Gratitude in leadership doesn't mean ignoring the hard stuff.
It means refusing to let it have the final say.

If you want to change a school, start by changing what you celebrate. What you notice. What you name out loud.

Because what you look for—grows.

Why Gratitude Matters in Leadership

Gratitude isn't fluff. It's not a warm fuzzy bonus after the data dive. It's fuel. And the research backs it up.

Brain scans show that practicing gratitude activates the prefrontal cortex, responsible for decision-making, empathy, and emotional regulation. It also increases dopamine and serotonin, the feel-good chemicals that support mood, resilience, and sleep.

According to neuroscientist Alex Korb, focusing on gratitude can automatically rewire the brain to search for the positive. That's a leadership superpower.

But gratitude doesn't just change brain chemistry. It changes culture chemistry.

It builds trust.
It signals to belong.
It reminds people they are seen, valued, and essential.

The Cup Story

One of my favorite analogies:
You're holding a cup of coffee when someone bumps into you. What spills out? Coffee. Not because someone hit you—but because that's what was in the cup.

Translation? What's inside of you spills out when life bumps into you. And it will.

So ask yourself: What's in your cup?

When the day unravels, when someone misses their duty again, and when the stress hits, what spills out? Gratitude? Patience? Bitterness? Cynicism?

We can't always choose our circumstances. But we can choose what we fill ourselves with. And I want my cup brimming with grace and thankfulness.

Because I promise—it will spill.

What Gratitude Looks Like in a School

Gratitude in leadership isn't performative. It's intentional.

It lives in small, sacred moments:

- A sticky note that says, "I saw how you handled that tough moment today. You're amazing."
- A public shout-out in a staff meeting for the teammate who holds everyone together.
- A handwritten card after a hard week.
- A warm hallway hug (consent-based, of course).

Gratitude doesn't stop the storm but anchors us to each other in the middle of it.

Gratitude as a Culture-Builder

Want to shift your school culture? Start with your language.

These eight phrases, inspired by Justin Wright, are some of the most powerful tools you can embed into your leadership vocabulary:

- I trust you.
- Thank you.
- You've got this.
- I'm here for you.
- I made a mistake.
- That's okay. We can fix it.
- Your ideas are valuable.
- What's your perspective?

They seem simple. But they're not small. They are signals—what Daniel Coyle calls "belonging cues." They tell people: You matter here. You are safe here. You belong here.

These words don't just feel good. They build the foundation for innovation, collaboration, feedback, and risk-taking. Because where there's trust, there's movement. And where there's gratitude, there's trust.

Gratitude Is Contagious—and Strategic

Gratitude doesn't just feel good. It spreads.

In The Culture Code, Daniel Coyle shares that a simple thank-you can spark a cascade of generosity and trust. These small signals—what he calls "belonging cues"—shift people's behavior. They increase collaboration, risk-taking, and connection.

Think about it: When did you give your best to someone who never noticed?

Now flip it: What would you do for someone who truly saw your effort?

That's the power of gratitude.

It's not about being nice. It's about being intentional.

As a leader, you have the power to set that tone. Once you do, it becomes contagious because people who feel appreciated naturally pass it on.

Gratitude Practices That Stick

Over the years, we've embedded gratitude into the fabric of our school—not as a one-time event, but as a rhythm.

One of our favorites is the gratitude Journals and Gratitude Walls in the staff lounge. Colleagues leave handwritten notes of appreciation or encouragement, and reading them is an instant mood-lifter—it's like walking into a hallway of high-fives.

We start every staff meeting with five minutes of celebrations—wins big and small, a breakthrough with a student, a funny hallway moment, someone showing up with joy after a tough week. It shifts the energy and reminds us who we are.

After every major event or project, I send Thank-You Texts. These are quick, specific messages about a lesson nailed, a student calmed, or a moment that mattered.

We also keep a Staff Favorites Book—a binder filled with each staff member's preferences—snacks, drinks, hobbies—little details that make it easy to celebrate people personally and meaningfully.

And then there are my Gratitude Rounds. I set a timer. I walk the building. I pop into classrooms and name something I saw that made a difference.

Not to evaluate. Just to say thank you.

None of these routines take much time, and I wish I could say I do them every day without missing them, but that's not true. However, when I do... the impact is immeasurable.

The Science Says... Gratitude Makes You Tougher

According to the Greater Good Science Center at UC Berkeley, gratitude isn't just good—it's protective. It improves psychological health, boosts emotional resilience, and strengthens mental stamina.

One study showed that veterans with higher levels of gratitude experienced significantly lower rates of PTSD.

We're not on a battlefield, but let's be honest: School leadership has its share of emotional landmines.

Gratitude becomes armor—not the kind that hardens us, but the kind that shields us with perspective and steadies us through the chaos. It doesn't ignore the stress. It outweighs it.

And if brain science says gratitude helps us sleep better, regulate emotions, and make better decisions... then yes, please. I'll take all of that.

Gratitude isn't a soft skill. It's a survival strategy.

Mirror Moment: Fill the Cup

Leadership is pressure. The bumps, bruises, last-minute emails, and "Can I talk to you for just a second?" moments stretch into twenty.

Some days, you're steady. On other days, you're spilling everywhere. That's why it matters what you're filled with.

So take a breath. And ask yourself:
- What am I filling myself with today?
- Who needs to hear "thank you" from me right now?
- How can I lead with gratitude—not just feel it quietly but show it boldly?

And then—fill up. Pour it out. Spill it everywhere. Because appreciation isn't just a nice idea, it's necessary.

And the people in your building? They don't need a perfect leader. They need a present one—one filled with something worth sharing.

Practical Strategy: "The Gratitude Ripple"

If you want to create a culture of appreciation, start a ripple.

Here's how:

At the beginning of a staff meeting, surprise one team member with a handwritten note of appreciation and a small token—maybe a favorite snack, a coffee gift card, or a simple treat.

Be specific. "I saw how you helped that student reset yesterday. That took patience, heart, and skill. Thank you for showing up like that." Then, that staff member has 48 hours to pay it forward to someone else in the building. The only rule? Be thoughtful, sincere, and personal.

Track the ripple. Create a bulletin board or digital display where each recipient adds their name and a brief note about what it meant to them. Over time, this becomes a visible web of connection—a celebration of how people see and support one another.

And while the snacks are nice, something more profound is happening behind the scenes:

Gratitude increases dopamine and serotonin. It strengthens social bonds. It rewires our brains to scan for what's right, not just what's wrong.

You're not just passing a compliment.
You're building trust.
You're shaping culture.
You're making joy a team sport.

Staff Shout-Outs That Stick (and Spread)

Our Staff Shout-Outs is one of the simplest, most powerful tools we use to build culture.

These aren't whispered compliments in passing—they're loud, proud, and public. Each edition of our staff newsletter features shout-outs for teammates who've gone above and beyond. Maybe they supported a student, covered for a colleague, or brought great energy into the building when we all needed it.

But we don't stop there.

At our monthly school-wide assemblies, we read the shout-outs aloud—in front of students, families, and the entire school. We even give out real certificates with fun fonts and a little flair. You'd be amazed how many staff members hang them on their doors, post them on social media, or send pictures to their families. Why? Because it matters to be seen. Not just by your principal but by the people you serve alongside—and the students you pour into daily. Recognition doesn't have to be expensive. But it *has* to be real.

Brain science backs it up. Public appreciation activates the brain's reward system, boosts motivation, and increases oxytocin, the connection chemical. It also models something. When kids see teachers celebrated for kindness, consistency, and teamwork—not just test scores or tough love—they learn what matters in a community.

Gratitude doesn't just spread. It multiplies.

Gratitude Is More Than a Gesture—It's a Leadership Strategy

Gratitude isn't a soft skill. It's not an add-on, a perk, or a box to check once a quarter. It's leadership. It's brain-based, heart-centered, culture-shaping work.

When practiced consistently and authentically, gratitude builds trust, strengthens resilience, and fuels connection. It rewires our brains, lifts people from burnout, and helps teams withstand the weight of heavy seasons.

GRATITUDE ISN'T FLUFF—IT'S FUEL. IT REWIRES BRAINS AND SHIFTS TEAMS.

And here's the truth: We can't afford not to lead with gratitude.

Our teams are tired. The work is hard. But when people feel seen, known, and valued, they stay—not because they need applause, but because they need to know they matter. Gratitude doesn't just impact the person who receives it. It transforms the one who gives it. It shifts our focus from what's broken to what's working, from what's missing to what's already showing up strong. It makes us slower to judge and quicker to celebrate.

So, hand out the certificates, read the names, clap loudly, and cheer hard. When we celebrate our people well, we build a culture where everyone knows their effort has an impact. Ultimately, it's not the spreadsheets or initiatives that make a school thrive—it's the relationships.

Gratitude is how we tend to them.

It doesn't make the work easier.
It makes it *worth it.*

Leadership Soundtrack: From Joy to Legacy

Track 8: "Gratitude" – Brandon Lake

"So I throw up my hands and praise you again and again / 'Cause all that I have is a hallelujah..."

Leadership isn't always loud. Sometimes, it whispers in small, faithful moments—a handwritten note, a hallway high-five, a quiet presence when someone needs it most. It doesn't need fanfare to matter. It needs heart.

Gratitude grounds us when the weight of this work feels too heavy.

It pulls us back to what's true, to the sacredness of showing up— again and again—with humility, hope, and a hallelujah in our soul.

It's not weakness—it's our strength.

It keeps us soft when the world gets sharp.

It reminds us to lead with reverence for the people, not just the plan.

When we model that kind of thankfulness—raw, real, and rooted in love—we don't just build better schools.

We build better legacies.

The next chapter leads you into love.

Not the polished kind.

The kind that sticks around. That fuels joy. That shows up, especially on the hard days.

Because in the end, leadership is less about the spotlight—and more about how we show up when no one's watching.

And those who lead with love?

They leave behind more than results.

They leave behind light.

And when we lead with appreciation—loudly, consistently, and without conditions—we don't just create momentum.

We create a legacy.

The next chapter invites you into that love.
Not the fluffy kind.
The fierce kind.

THE LEADERS WHO LOVE WELL? THEY LEAVE MORE THAN RESULTS.

The kind that stays. That believes. That builds people—on their best days and their worst ones.

Because, in the end, leadership isn't just about what you do. It's about how you make people feel.

And the leaders who love well? They leave more than results. They leave light.

CHAPTER 9

Lead with Love. Fuel with Joy

"JOY IS NOT IN THINGS; IT IS IN US."- RICHARD WAGNER

When Joy Stops Being Optional

Let's be honest: this job is not for the faint.

Leadership will stretch your soul, test your limits, and demand more than you sometimes think you have left to give. People can be complicated. Emotions are messy. And the days are long.

But joy?

Joy is the secret sauce.

It makes the hard days bearable and the good ones unforgettable.

JOY IS THE SECRET SAUCE.

Early on, I thought being a "real" principal meant staying serious and stoic. Clipboard in hand.

Deep-in-thought face. I even practiced that thoughtful nod in the mirror. (Yikes.)

But then joy found me—on a cart.

When Joy Crashed My Clipboard

Our building stood after the tornado, but our spirit sagged. Teachers were drained, and students were unsettled. I was running on caffeine and autopilot. The air felt heavy with unspoken exhaustion.

Then came Mrs. Kilby.

She barreled down the hallway, music blasting, sunglasses on, her cart squeaking like a grocery aisle dance party. I should've said something principal-like. Something OSHA-related, probably.

Instead, I jumped on the cart.

Yes—heels, blazer, all of it. Full principal joyride.

We filled it with treats, notes, bubble wands, and whatever ridiculous treasure we could find in the lounge or my stash. Then we cranked the volume, grabbed the walkie-talkie, and turned that hallway into a parade route.

And something shifted. Teachers smiled. Kids peeked out of classrooms. Laughter bounced off the freshly patched walls. That moment reminded me that joy doesn't distract from the work—it carries it. That day, I stopped treating joy like a luxury and started treating it like a leadership strategy—not the kind you put in a data tracker, but the kind that holds the whole thing together.

Since then? Flash mob dance breaks. Theme day costumes. Rubber duck scavenger hunts. April Fool's pranks (sorry, team). Peep wars. Sonic drink Fridays. All of it.

Because when you choose joy on purpose, you give your people permission to exhale, connect, and believe that—even in the hardest seasons—there's still light to be found.

And sometimes, that light rides a squeaky cart with a Bluetooth speaker and a principal who forgot she was supposed to be professional.

Thank goodness for that.

The Courage to Lead with Love

Love is not the opposite of leadership. It is leadership.

Let's be clear: leading with love isn't soft. It isn't fluff. And it certainly isn't naïve. It's presence. It's noticing. It's choosing people—on purpose—again and again.

Love shows up in the hallway with a hug, in a text that says, "Thinking of you, " in a calendar reminder to ask how that surgery went, and in a note on a tough day that simply reads, "You're doing better than you think."

It shows up with Sonic drinks on a Friday and Shrek ears when a kid dares you to. It shows up on classroom floors, car rides, retirement parties, baby showers, and all the messy, beautiful spaces in between these things.

But love also shows up in the hard conversations. It looks like gently asking, "How are you really doing?" And sometimes, it looks like walking someone toward help when they're too tired to ask for it themselves.

After one of the hardest seasons of my leadership life, I started seeing a counselor. I didn't announce it, and I didn't plan for anyone to know, but word got out. And what happened next floored me.

Staff came to me—quietly, privately—and said, "Thank you. If you can do it, I think I can, too."

That's when I realized that modeling care isn't about appearances. It's about creating space for healing.

Because when I care for myself, I lead from wholeness, not depletion.

That, too, is love. And no, it's not soft. It's the fiercest, most transformative leadership tool I know.

Mirror Moment: What Does Fun Look Like in Your School?

Take a mental walk through your building—the lounge, the hallways, the meeting room. Do they feel hopeful? Playful? Connected? Where is joy already taking root, and where is it missing?

Now ask yourself:
- What small tradition could you start this week to remind your staff this place is special?
- What could you do to make your people smile before 8 a.m.?
- What kind of fun is missing that only you can give permission for?

This isn't about adding more. It's about making space for what already matters.

It's joy—on purpose.

Practical Strategy: Building a Culture of Joy & Connection

Joy isn't surface-level. It's soul-level. And connection isn't a break from the work—it's what helps us do the work.

Building a joyful, connected school culture isn't about grand gestures. It's about tiny, intentional rhythms that whisper to your team, "You matter. This place matters."

Try one or more of these:

Set the tone with human moments.
Start staff meetings with five minutes of real talk. Ask, "What's something that made you laugh this week?" or "What's a high and a hope you're carrying?" These moments cut through the noise and remind us we're people before professionals.

Weave joy into weekly routines.
Create micro-traditions like "Two-Minute Tuesdays," where staff can anonymously submit wins to be read aloud, or "Desk Fairy Days," where a small note or treat mysteriously appears on a random desk— no explanation, just delight.

Track and celebrate joy visibly.
Set up a Joy Board. Ask staff and students to post moments of kindness, laughter, or encouragement. Keep it updated. Let it grow into living proof that the good stuff is always happening.

Create surprise & delight moments.

Drop an impromptu breakfast bar in the lounge, cue up a dance break over the intercom, and post a pop-up gratitude wall. These simple, unexpected gestures say, "We take our work seriously—but not ourselves."

Build in reflective joy.
Every now and then, ask your team, "What brought you joy this week?" Let them share—on a whiteboard, in a PLC, or even in a group thread. Joy that's named becomes joy that sticks.

Joy doesn't just appear—it's cultivated.

The more intentionally you plant it, the more it blooms—especially when your people need it most.

Love Is the Legacy

Joy isn't a break from the work. It is the work.

It's how we carry the pressure. It's how we build trust. It's how we remind our people—and ourselves—that this isn't just a job.

It's a calling.

And yes, sometimes that calling comes wrapped in a chicken suit with a Bluetooth speaker and a hallway full of laughter.

But here's the truth:
The fun isn't a distraction. It's a declaration.

It says, *"We can do hard things and still hold onto each other."*

It says, *"You're not alone here."*

It says, "Even now—especially now—this work is still good."

So lead with joy. Love loud. And never underestimate the power of a squeaky cart and a well-timed playlist.

Leadership Soundtrack: From the Parking Lot to Purpose

Track 9: "Humble and Kind" – Tim McGraw

"When those dreams you're dreamin' come to you / When the work you put in is realized / Let yourself feel the pride, but always stay humble and kind..."

Leadership doesn't begin in boardrooms. It begins in parking lots, at bus duty, in grocery store run-ins, and on doorsteps—where trust is built, one quiet moment at a time.

Because leadership is never just about your voice.
It's about how many voices you help others find.

And joy? Joy is what carries them forward.
Love is what anchors them in place.
That's the legacy.

The next chapter asks the question every culture-builder must eventually face: Now that you've found your footing, how do you help others rise, too? Because great leaders don't just stand tall. They lift others as they climb.

Part 3:

From Teams to Trust

CHAPTER 10

Start in the Parking Lot

"LEADERSHIP DOESN'T BEGIN WITH A GRAND OPENING OR AN ANNOUNCEMENT IN THE NEWSPAPER. SOMETIMES, IT STARTS IN A DOLLAR GENERAL PARKING LOT."

The Parking Lot Welcome

It was summer. I was new to town and the role, trying to get a feel for the community I was about to lead. With little open and fewer choices, I found myself at Dollar General—THE Dollar General.

As I stepped out of my car, a voice cut through the heat:
"Are you the new principal?"

No school shirt. No badge. No clipboard. Just me, in regular clothes. I turned. "Yes, ma'am."

She didn't miss a beat.
"You'll do just fine here—so long as you listen and don't act like you're better than us."

That was it. That was the whole conversation.
And it marked the beginning of everything.

She didn't know me—but she saw me. She reminded me that respect here had to be earned. Not with credentials. Not with titles. But with humility, presence, and genuine connection.

I stayed in her good graces for all ten years I served in that role. And trust me—I never wanted to find out what the alternative looked like.

Why Community Matters

It's easy to get consumed by lesson plans, walkthroughs, and district reports. The inbox fills up. The to-do list never ends. And somewhere along the way, it's tempting to forget a core truth:

Schools don't exist in isolation. They are living, breathing parts of the communities they serve. Strong schools are built on strong relationships—not just with students and staff but also with families, neighborhoods, churches, grocery clerks, and front porch conversations.

Family engagement isn't a checkbox. It's not just a carnival in October or a newsletter in someone's backpack.

It's built-in and consistent presence.
In showing up.
In asking, "What matters to you?" and actually listening to the answer.

The most transformative seasons of my leadership haven't come from a new program or strategy. They've come from relationships—deep, mutual trust between school and family. Whether it was a Family Wellness Night, a parent-led project, or a simple pickup line conversation, the more we invested in families, the more they invested in us.

When families feel like they belong, they begin to believe that school success isn't just for some kids—it's for theirs, too.

From Judgment to Connection

That woman in the Dollar General parking lot didn't tell me how to run a school—she told me how to be human.

Her words reminded me that we can't lead people we don't understand and that we can't understand people we don't talk to.

So, I started showing up. There were spaghetti dinners at the church, grocery store run-ins, and conversations in the bleachers. I left the office and stepped into the community.

Engagement doesn't follow our schedule—it follows our presence. It happens in the unscripted moments, the "Hey, how's your mom doing?" check-ins, the porch hellos, and the grace in the gaps.

Sidebar: Parking Lot Ministry

Some of my most meaningful leadership moments haven't happened in my office. They've happened in parking lots, on porches, and leaning over the hoods of cars.

That's where trust lives.

Sometimes, the parents who seem the most distant carry the heaviest load. The ones who seem angry or disengaged are often scared, overwhelmed, or unsure how to help. If we lead with judgment, we miss the moment. But if we lead with curiosity and grace, we open the door to something deeper.

Connection doesn't require perfection. It requires presence.

They Don't Show Up

We've all heard it. Maybe we've even said it.
"Parents just don't care."
"They never show up."
"They're not involved."

But what if we stopped assuming apathy—and started asking about access?

Maybe they didn't come because they're working two jobs. Because they've never had a positive school experience. Because they're worried, they won't understand the paperwork—or be understood at all. Maybe they didn't show up... because they weren't sure they'd be welcomed when they did.

The truth is that families carry more than we see. And sometimes, what looks like disinterest is fear, fatigue, or generational hurt.

As a staff, we started naming our assumptions out loud.

Instead of asking, "Why don't they care?" we asked, "What barriers might be in their way?"

That one shift—just that question—opened the door to empathy, inclusive strategies, and stronger relationships.

Because mindset matters.
If we lead with judgment, we shut people out.
But if we lead with grace, we build bridges.

And sometimes, all it takes to change everything is one remembered relationship... or one unexpected act of kindness.

Cultural Responsiveness and Honoring Diversity

Authentic engagement means meeting families where they are—and honoring who they are.

Language barriers, cultural differences, work schedules, and family dynamics all influence how and when families engage with school. If we're serious about connection, we have to be serious about understanding those realities.

AUTHENTIC ENGAGEMENT MEANS MEETING FAMILIES WHERE THEY ARE—AND HONORING WHO THEY ARE.

We started by asking simple but powerful questions: How do you prefer to be contacted? What time works for your family? What would make you feel more welcome?

Then we listened—and made changes. We translated materials. We used apps that supported multilingual messaging. We included representation from all backgrounds in our communication, events, and visuals during multicultural month and all year.

We examined our events, too. Were they accessible to working families? Did they reflect the community's diversity? Were we creating space for families to feel seen—or unintentionally leaving them out?

Inclusion isn't a theme. It's a practice. Not a checklist, but a lens. It's built on empathy, intentionality, and the willingness to keep learning.

Balancing Leadership and Parenthood

I can't talk about family engagement without talking about my own.

Being a mom while leading a school is the most beautiful, complex, and guilt-ridden part of my journey. Some seasons brought deep joy and connection, while others brought me to my knees in exhaustion and doubt.

I'll never forget the image of my first grader asleep under my desk—curled up next to my kicked-off heels after a long day. That's real. That's raw. That's the collision of leadership and motherhood.

It's not just about the missed moments at home. It's about the emotional weight of giving so much to others while feeling like you're giving less to your own.

But here's what I've learned: having my kids in my school was also my most powerful reminder of why I lead.

Every decision, call, and policy I questioned was filtered through one question: **Would I want this for my child?** This lens sharpened my leadership, making me more compassionate, protective, thoughtful, and fierce.

Still, it's okay to name the tension. It's okay to say you're tired. And it's necessary to give yourself permission—to rest, reset, and return.

Because leadership and motherhood don't cancel each other out. They deepen each other.

Boundaries and Balance

Now, let's name the thing no one wants to say out loud: Burnout is real. And if you're not careful, family engagement can become another place you give until there's nothing left.

I learned—honestly, the hard way—that being present doesn't mean being available 24/7. So, I started setting boundaries. I stopped answering emails after a certain hour. I gave myself space to decompress after heavy meetings. I modeled balance for my staff—not just in what I said, but in how I lived.

Our families do need us, but they need us whole and not hollowed out. They don't deserve to see us only running on fumes—not so emotionally depleted that our presence feels like a performance.

The best thing you can give your school community is your whole self. And that means honoring your limits, protecting your peace, and giving yourself the same grace you extend to everyone else. It's not selfish. It's sustainable. And sustainable leadership is what keeps you—and your school—standing.

Inspiration: When the Community Becomes the Mission

Schools thrive when the community becomes more than an audience—when it becomes the **mission.** When parents aren't just invited to events, but empowered as partners. When stakeholders have a seat at the table, not just a spot on the mailing list. When relationships lead the way—not as a supplement, but as the spark behind it all.

Real school improvement isn't just about test scores or pacing guides. It's about trust—between schools and families, teachers and parents, leaders and communities. And that kind of trust? It's built in moments. In small hellos. In remembered names. In quiet acts of dignity. It's not grand. It's consistent.

Because when families feel like they're in it with you—not just watching from the outside—everything changes. Your school becomes ours. Your mission becomes theirs. And the future becomes something you build—*together*.

The Ripple Effect of a Relationship

There was a day I'll never forget—what we thought would be a routine home visit turned into a story that still gives me goosebumps.

My counselor and I had an address scribbled on a sticky note. One of our students had missed several school days, and we planned a quick check-in. But we knocked on the wrong door.

A mother answered. Five children peeked out from behind her. None of them were enrolled in school.

Not one.

They hadn't fallen through the cracks—they'd never even been near the system. This wasn't just about truancy. This was about access, awareness, and survival.

She didn't know how to enroll them.
She didn't know where to start.
And then, something remarkable happened.

She looked at my counselor, Mrs. Kilby, and said, "You were my teacher.""

In that moment, everything changed.

A remembered kindness cracked open a door much wider than the one we had knocked on. That simple recognition—*you saw me once, and I still remember*—became the bridge to trust.

We enrolled every child, coordinated services—transportation, meals, supplies, and medical support—and connected the family with GED resources. Eventually, the mother found the courage to leave an unsafe home environment.

All because of a door we hadn't meant to knock on. All because of a relationship formed years earlier that still had ripple effects.

I'll be honest—home visits used to make me uncomfortable. I loved the structure of school. But stepping into someone's life? That felt messy. Unscripted. Hard to control.

But Mrs. Kilby, my co-leader in that work, was fearless and didn't hesitate. She reminded me that the most transformational leadership sometimes happens outside the building.

On porches.
In driveways.
Over the sound of kids laughing in the background.

We fed pets, treated lice, packed hotel rooms, and made sure people didn't feel invisible.

She used to joke, "We're just out here savin' lives." But it wasn't really a joke. She did.

She's still doing it—in another district now, blessing another community. But the impact of how she led still shapes how I lead today.

Titles or tasks don't measure real leadership; it's measured by how we show up. By the moments when kindness echoes louder than strategy—and still leaves a mark.

Mirror Moment: The Family Engagement & Action Planner

Part 1: Self-Reflection
Take a moment to reflect honestly on your current approach to family engagement.
- What's working?
- What's not?
- What assumptions about families and their involvement might exist—personally or school-wide?

Have you ever thought or heard someone say: *"They just don't care."* or *"They never show up."*

Now, think of one family you've struggled to connect with. What barrier might be at play that isn't immediately visible? What could shift if you looked through the lens of empathy, not assumption?

Part 2: Cultural Responsiveness Inventory
✓ Check the strategies you already use.
☆ Star two that you want to implement this year.

___Provide translated materials and multilingual communication tools.

___ Ask families how they prefer to be contacted.

___ Host culturally relevant events (food, language, holidays, etc.).

___ Include diverse voices and stories in classroom materials and displays.

___ Survey families on what events or support they'd find most helpful.

Part 3: "Five Families" Mapping Activity
Choose five families from your school who may not be regularly engaged. Without making assumptions, brainstorm one way to connect more meaningfully with each: *What would it look like if family engagement wasn't a strategy but a mindset?*

 ## Practical Strategy: Relationship-First Outreach

If we want engagement to be authentic, we have to go where the relationships live. It's not about better flyers or fancier events—it's about presence, empathy, and shared space.

Here are a few ways to reimagine outreach through a relational lens:

- **Home visits** that aren't punitive or reactive—but proactive, relational, and rooted in learning families' stories.
- **Coffee chats with the principal** are held off campus—at parks, libraries, or the parking lot in a couple of lawn chairs. They are simple, human, and approachable.
- **Family goal-setting conferences** where students, families, and teachers co-create goals—turning conferences into conversations.
- **Open-door days** where families observe learning in action—not just on showcase nights, but in real-time.
- **Community walks** are when school staff walk neighborhoods, knock on doors, and offer presence without an agenda—just connection.

The 3 Cs of Relationship-First Family Engagement:

Consistency – Make outreach a habit, not a one-time push. When communication is regular and personal, trust grows.

Curiosity – Ask questions with a genuine desire to understand. What matters to your families? What makes them feel included?

Celebration – Call home with good news more than bad news. Celebrate growth, effort, and kindness—not just academic wins.

These strategies require time, flexibility, and a little courage. But the return is worth it.

When families feel seen and valued, they become more than supporters—they become partners. And those partnerships don't just strengthen schools—they transform them.

They turn your students into *our* students. They turn school improvement into community transformation.

The Power of One Conversation

The woman in the Dollar General parking lot may never know how much she shaped me.

But her message still rings in my heart: Be honest, be present, and never think you're above the people you serve.

Leadership isn't built in boardrooms; it's built in everyday spaces. In how you greet someone. In how you listen. Whether or not you make people feel like they matter.

So, lead with humility.
Lead with presence.
Lead from the edge.

And never underestimate the power of one unexpected, unforgettable conversation.

Leadership Soundtrack: The Courage to Begin Again

Track 10: "Brand New" – Ben Rector

"Like a heartbeat skip, like an open page / Like a one-way trip on an airplane... It's a brand new day."

Sometimes, leadership begins in a parking lot.

And sometimes, it begins all over again—after a crisis, a culture shift, or a moment when everything you thought was steady falls apart. What comes next isn't always easy. But it's often necessary.

The next chapter invites you to rediscover your footing—to rebuild a team, a mission, or maybe even your sense of self.

And you're not starting from scratch.
You're starting from experience.

And that makes all the difference.

Beginning Again

The first time we started over, it was forced—after the tornado. The second time, it was a choice—a decision to rebuild not just a building but a culture. Starting over doesn't always mean a blank slate. Sometimes, it means looking around and realizing what used to work doesn't anymore.

It means facing burnout and naming the disconnection. And choosing to build something better—together.

We weren't just recovering from a storm. We were recovering from turnover, trauma, and a fractured sense of mission. The effort was still there—but the spark had dimmed.

We needed more than a reset. We needed *renewal*. And it had to start with a shift from "me" to "we."

Building a Team-First Mindset

Our first step was to redefine what "team" really meant. It wasn't about shared lunchrooms or meeting obligations. It was about shared accountability, shared purpose, and shared wins. Teachers, custodians, paras, and specialists needed to feel part of something bigger.

Our new mantra became: "No one does this alone." We embraced shared leadership, not in title, but in action. We invited everyone to lead—facilitating PLCs, mentoring colleagues, guiding book studies, or simply being the go-to person for a strategy or resource.
Then we asked a bold question: What kind of team do we want to be?

We handed out sticky notes at a staff meeting and asked every person to write down five words that described their ideal team. The responses were raw, honest, and full of hope: trusting, supportive, growth-minded, kind, and accountable.

From there, our leadership team sifted through the notes and narrowed the list to five core words—our cultural compass moving forward.

Sidebar: The Sticky Note Wall

We printed those five words on butcher paper and hung them outside the staff lounge. Nothing fancy—just intention taped to the wall. Then, something small but powerful happened.

One teacher added sticky notes each Friday: "Thanks for your kindness today.", "I appreciated your grit with that tough class.", "You helped me breathe this week."

Within weeks, the wall bloomed—layered with color, encouragement, and connection.

It became a mirror—not of who we were, but who we were becoming.

Those five words weren't decorations. They became anchors. We used them to guide hiring, coaching, conversations, and celebrations. They weren't slogans—they were signals. This is who we are. This is how we lead.

Some staff got teary. Others said, "This is the first time I've ever been asked to dream about my team."

That's when we knew that culture doesn't begin with policy. It begins with permission to hope, to speak, and to build something better together.

These five words became our anchor. We printed them on posters, used them to guide hiring decisions, brought them into coaching conversations and team meetings, and, most importantly, modeled them daily. Some staff got teary. Others said it was the first time they'd been asked to dream about what kind of team they wanted to be.

That wall reminded us that culture isn't built overnight—it's built one small moment at a time. Sticky note by sticky note. Word by word. It taught me that leadership is less about control and more about creating space—for others to rise, to connect, to lead. What started as five hopeful words became a living reflection of who we were becoming. And just when it felt like we had found our rhythm, life invited me to begin again—this time, not just with a team, but within myself.

Another Fresh Start—A Leap into the Unknown

Laying a new foundation took on a whole new meaning when I made one of the boldest leadership moves of my career. After ten years at a school I loved, I stepped into the unknown:

New school. New model. New state. New everything.

I didn't know a soul. I hadn't hired the team. The students, the families—even the neighborhood—were unfamiliar.

It wasn't just uncharted territory. It was a blank canvas. And I had to lead without the comfort of history or trust already built.

I still remember what nudged me forward.

My personal counselor—who had walked with me through so many storms—looked at me and said, "It's time for you to start making decisions again." She wasn't talking about logistics or lesson plans. She meant me. She had seen something I hadn't yet admitted: I had stopped leading boldly. I had stopped moving forward. I was stuck in survival mode—safe, steady, and playing small.

Her words landed like lightning.

It was time. Time to move. Time to grow. Time to lead from the edge again.

Leaving wasn't easy. It meant letting go of comfort and familiarity—of being known.

It meant stepping into a system I didn't build, with a team I didn't choose, and a culture I had to create from the ground up. I'm not going to lie—there were moments in those first few weeks when I thought I was being punked. I questioned everything. My choices. My voice. My capacity. I sent more than one text to my husband, warning that we might have to sell the house because I would be fired by Friday. (Spoiler: I wasn't.)

But here's the truth about beginning again: It's not weak. It's not failure. It's *bravery in motion*. It's choosing to rise—again—even when no one sees the struggle. It's choosing to lead, even when it would be easier to play small. Because courage doesn't live in certainty; it lives in motion.

The Five Words Exercise

When you're trying to rebuild culture—especially from scratch—clarity is everything. We returned to one of our leadership toolbox's simplest, most powerful tools: the Five Words exercise.

Reflect with your team: "If someone were to describe *our* team in five words, what would they say?" Then flip the script: "What five words *should* describe us?" "What do we want it to feel like to work here, teach here, lead here?"

And then ask: **What do we need to do to make those words accurate?**

Here's how it works:

1. Prompt your staff to write down five words that describe their ideal team culture.
2. Break into small groups and discuss. Let them find common themes together.
3. As a leadership team, gather all the responses and identify the top five words that align with your school's mission and values.
4. Share them publicly. Post them. Use them. Say them out loud often.
5. Let those words guide everything:
    - Hiring decisions
    - Coaching conversations
    - Team norms
    - Professional learning
    - Daily interactions

When teams help define who they want to become, they *own* the transformation. They see themselves not just as participants—but as *co-creators* of culture. It's not a strategy.

It's a stake in the ground.

Mirror Moment

How are you creating space for others to lead? Think about your team. Who's stepping forward with ideas? Who's quietly waiting to be invited? Are you offering true opportunities—not just tasks—for people to lead?

Ask yourself:
- Am I empowering others to shape our direction?
- Are there voices missing from key decisions?
- What might shift if I stepped back just a little... and someone else stepped in?

Sometimes, leadership isn't about saying more—it's about *inviting more voices to the table.*

Practical Strategy: Leadership Decision-Making Reflection

When you're facing a tough decision—especially in the middle of a fresh start—pause and reflect before moving forward. Consider what values matter most in the moment and how your choice might impact your team, your students, and the culture you're trying to build. Ask yourself whether you're choosing the easy path or the right one, and who you can turn to for wisdom or perspective. Most importantly, consider whether this is a decision you'll be proud of five years from now.

Write the answers down. Talk them out loud. Whatever you do—own them because leadership isn't about never doubting. It's about deciding with clarity, consistency, and care.

Beginning Again Is Not a Failure

STARTING OVER IS NOT A SIGN THAT YOU'VE FAILED. IT'S PROOF THAT YOU'VE GROWN.

Starting over is not a sign that you've failed. It's proof that you've grown.

It's an invitation to build something stronger, more aligned, and more sustainable than what came before. Shared leadership isn't just a way to lighten your load.

It's a mindset for transformation.

When we invite others in—into the work, into the why, into the decisions—we don't lose control.
We gain capacity.
We gain trust.
We gain a team that owns the vision right alongside us.

So whether you're starting fresh in a new school, rebuilding a fractured culture, or simply choosing to reset how you lead—know this: **You're not back at the beginning**. You're just beginning again—with experience, wisdom, and heart.

Leadership Soundtrack: From Falling Forward to Rising Together

Track 11: "Try Everything" – Shakira

"Birds don't just fly / They fall down and get up / Nobody learns without getting it wrong..."

Starting over isn't weakness—it's wisdom. It's leadership that's honest enough to say, "This isn't working," and brave enough to try again.

The next chapter moves from recommitment to **resilience**—not the kind built on hustle, but the kind rooted in gratitude, perspective, and the quiet strength to keep showing up.

Because what we name, we nurture. And what we nurture? That's what lasts.

CHAPTER 12

Finding the Good

"YOU GET MORE OF WHAT YOU LOOK FOR."

Some chapters aren't planned. They emerge—not from curriculum maps or strategic initiatives, but from the hallway smiles, the shared laughs in the teacher lounge, and the whispered "thank you" from a student who finally feels seen. This chapter is about those moments—finding the good—not because everything is perfect, but because it isn't.

As leaders, we spend a lot of time solving problems, looking for gaps, reviewing data, and managing crises. If we're not careful, we forget to look for what's working, growing, and quietly holding it together.

Joy isn't an afterthought. It's a leadership strategy. And if you want a culture that thrives, you have to name the good on purpose.

Reframing the Lens

We know your brain is Velcro for the negative and Teflon for the positive. This biological survival trait doesn't serve us well in leadership.

The good news? You can retrain your brain. Research in neuroscience and positive psychology shows that regularly noticing, naming, and reflecting on positive experiences changes your brain's default wiring. It builds resilience, optimism, and connection.

And the best part? It spreads. Emotional tone is contagious— especially when you're the one people look to for direction.

The Sticky Note That Changed Everything

It was a Tuesday. It was one of those weeks when the calendar was overbooked, the tension was high, and the to-do list felt like a monster breathing down my neck. I was questioning everything: my impact, my energy, and whether I was even making a difference.

On my way back from a difficult parent meeting, I stopped at my office door and saw it: a sticky note in slanted handwriting, one sentence: "Thank you for making this place feel like home."

I don't know who wrote it, and I never found out, but it stopped me in my tracks.

I sat down, sticky note still in hand, and cried. Not because I was sad. But because I had forgotten. I had forgotten that even when you feel like falling short, someone sees you showing up.

From that day forward, I started a new practice: the "Look For It List." Every day, before I shut my laptop, I wrote down one moment of good. Some days, it was big. Most days, it was small. But it rewired how I ended each day, and it gave me just enough light to walk into the next one.

From Toxic Positivity to Intentional Joy

Let's be clear: this isn't about pretending things are fine when they're not. This isn't about ignoring pain or dismissing struggle. That's toxic positivity, and it's harmful.

This is about *truthful optimism*. It's about leading with hope that is rooted in reality.

Joy doesn't require you to deny the hard stuff. It invites you to hold both: *to be fully present in the mess* while still noticing the light that shines through it.

"We don't deny the storm. We dance in the rain."

WE DON'T DENY THE STORM.

WE DANCE IN THE RAIN.

Principal Jay in Detroit

Jayla Thomas stepped into leadership at a K–8 school in Detroit that had been labeled "failing" for six years in a row. The building's ceiling tiles were falling in. The staff lounge smelled like despair. And the culture? Fractured.

Her first initiative wasn't a data wall. It wasn't a curriculum overhaul. It was a whiteboard in the lounge titled:

"We Found the Good Today."

She started writing notes each morning: "Nia smiled for the first time in three weeks." or "Mr. Harris used student artwork in his lesson." or "Zero fights today!"

At first, the staff rolled their eyes. Then, they started adding their own. Sticky notes. Dry erase scribbles. Memes. Jokes. Victories.

The tone began to shift.

By the end of the semester, the whiteboard was overflowing, and so were their hearts. Test scores didn't change overnight, but the *energy* did. And energy is the first step toward transformation.

Practical Strategy: Naming the Good

The Gratitude Walk

Once a week, take a walk through your building for 15 minutes. No clipboard. No checklist. Just eyes and heart open. Name out loud what you see that is good.

Say it to a teacher. A student. The custodian. Yourself.

The Look for It List

Keep a small notebook or open a digital note. Title it: "*Look for the Good.*" Each day, write: One win, One laugh, One small act of kindness, One personal moment of peace

Watch what happens when you start ending your days this way.

Progress Parties

Schedule a celebration once a quarter. Bring snacks, play music, and share a slideshow of photos and quotes. Celebrate not just data but *effort.*

Ask: "What did we do this quarter that made a kid feel seen?"

Visual Wall of Joy

Set up a bulletin board, digital slideshow, or classroom door. Invite staff and students to post pictures, wins, or notes. Keep it fresh and visible.

Make the good *unignorable*.

Joy as a Leadership Strategy

Joy builds trust, increases resilience, fosters connection, and enhances retention. It is the heartbeat of a culture people want to belong to.

People don't remember every staff meeting, but they remember how they felt in your building. Leadership will never be easy, but it can be joyful—not all the time, not in every moment, but often enough to make it sustainable.

Find the good. Name it. Share it. Naming the good doesn't mean ignoring the hard. It means facing it with hope in your pocket. And that hope becomes your compass when the real work begins—when you're called to lead change that matters.

Because what you name, you nurture. And what you nurture? That's what grows. As we move forward, let's not just lead with strategy. Let's lead with *light*.

Leadership Soundtrack: From Light Within to Light Beyond

Track 12: "I Am Light" – India.Arie

"I am not the things my family did / I am not the voices in my head / I am not the pieces of the brokenness inside..."

Joy doesn't just change a room—it changes a rhythm. When we choose to name the good on purpose, we become leaders who shift the energy, not just manage it. The next chapter invites us to go one step further—not just holding the light but passing it on. Because the way you lead today becomes the way others lead tomorrow. And in that, your impact becomes a legacy.

Change is Hard, but You Were Built for It

Change is one of the few constants in education—and still one of the hardest things to lead.

You can have the data, the research, and the perfect plan and still face resistance that makes you question everything.

But here's the truth: Resistance doesn't mean you're doing something wrong. It means you're doing something that matters.

> RESISTANCE DOESN'T MEAN YOU'RE DOING SOMETHING WRONG.
> IT MEANS YOU'RE DOING SOMETHING THAT <u>MATTERS</u>.

A Change That Almost Broke Me

I once led a significant instructional shift—not just a new strategy but a total mindset transformation.

We moved to data-driven instruction, common formative assessments, weekly collaboration built into every grade level, and accountability systems that made it impossible to hide behind the status quo.

On paper, it was solid. In practice, it was *brutal.*
Teachers were overwhelmed. Meetings felt tense. There were tears. There were walkouts. And there were nights I cried, too. I questioned myself constantly: Was I pushing too hard? Was the cost too high?

But somewhere deep down, I knew this change was right.

And the tipping point came when a teacher pulled me aside and said, "I didn't think I could do this. But now I see my kids learning more than ever. Thank you for not giving up on us."

That moment reminded me that leadership isn't about avoiding discomfort. It's about walking through it—with purpose, patience, and belief.

Understanding the Stages of Change

If you want to lead change well, you have to understand how people move through it. Change is rarely linear, and people don't all start in the same place. That makes leadership challenging and sacred: You're not just pushing a plan forward; you're walking people through a process.

Here's a simplified look at the stages of change:
- **Pre-Contemplation** – "This isn't a problem."
- **Contemplation** – "Something might need to change."
- **Preparation** – "I'm getting ready to try."
- **Action** – "I'm doing the work."
- **Maintenance** – "This is just how we do things now."

You may be ready to sprint while someone else is still lacing up their shoes. That's not failure. That's normal. The work is guiding people forward—one step, one conversation, one insight at a time.

Not everyone is in the same stage at the same time, and that's where the real challenge of leadership lies. You may be ready to sprint while your team is still stretching at the starting line. That's okay. The work is to guide people forward, one step at a time.

A Real-Life Example

Imagine you're rolling out a new data-driven intervention system.

You're energized—it's a game changer. But during that first staff meeting, a teacher crosses their arms and says, "I've been doing it this way for 20 years." That's a sign they're in the pre-contemplation stage of change. Another teacher acknowledges the value but admits, "I see how this could help, but I'm overwhelmed." That's contemplation. After the meeting, someone stays behind to ask for resources—preparation.

Within weeks, they're testing new strategies and tracking data—action. By spring, they're mentoring peers and improving the system together—maintenance.

This is the real work of leading change: not dragging people forward, but recognizing where they are and helping them take the next right step.

Mirror Moment: Navigating Change with Intention

Every leader has a default setting when it comes to change. Some of us charge forward. Some freeze. Some over-plan. Some avoid it altogether. And others tighten their grip on control.

Before you can guide others through change, you must understand how *you* move through it.

Take a moment to reflect on a change you're currently leading—or one on the horizon. Walk yourself through this guided process:

1. Clarify the Change:
   • What exactly is changing?
   • Who will this impact the most?

2. Identify the "Why":
   • Why is this change necessary?
   • How does it align with our school's mission/vision?

3. Anticipate Resistance:
   • What concerns or fears might staff have?
   • Where might misalignment or misunderstanding show up?

4. Plan Your Response:
   • How will I communicate clearly and consistently?
   • What supports will I put in place?
   • How can I celebrate progress?

5. Reflect on Yourself:
   • What is my reaction to this change?
   • What do I need to stay grounded and lead with presence?

You don't need to have all the answers. But you *do* need to lead with clarity and empathy. Because when your people see you processing change with intention, they'll feel safer doing the same.

Comfort is Not a Promise; Support Is

Here's a hard but honest truth: We can't always promise comfort as leaders.

Change—real change—is uncomfortable. It stretches people, shakes routines, and challenges beliefs. But while we can't (or shouldn't) guarantee comfort, we can guarantee support. Support means standing beside your team, not above them. It means providing resources, encouragement, and emotional safety while they navigate new territory.

When we rolled out a new literacy curriculum, anxiety ran high. "This feels like learning to teach all over again," one teacher admitted. Instead of mandating full implementation by a calendar date, we slowed down. We hosted workshops, offered one-on-one coaching, shared materials, checked in, and showed up.

That same teacher later said, "This is hard. But at least I don't feel like I'm doing it alone." That's what support looks like—not removing every challenge but making sure your people never face it unsupported.

Leaders who stay present—who listen, adapt, and show up consistently—build trust that outlasts any single initiative. You don't have to promise ease. Just promise you won't disappear when things get hard.

That's what your people will remember.

Build Team Efficacy and Clarity Through Shared Values

Shared values are among the most effective ways to unite a team during change. These are not just words on a poster—they are beliefs named by the people doing the work.

Michael Fullan (2014) reminds us that "clarity and coherence" are essential for creating a unified school culture. When people know what they stand for—and see those values reflected in action—they lean in.

We started with a simple activity.

We asked staff to name the qualities that defined their ideal school environment. No prompts. Just voices. Just honesty.

The words poured out: respect, joy, growth, equity, collaboration.

From dozens of sticky notes and hallway conversations, we distilled those words down into five core values that felt *true to us*.

Then we did something important: We used them.

We printed them, posted them, and referenced them in staff meetings. We asked during planning, "Does this reflect our values?" We used them in hiring interviews, coaching cycles, and leadership conversations. Over time, these values became more than language— they became our culture's compass.

When people see that decisions are rooted in what they helped define, they shift from compliance to commitment. They don't just *follow* the change. They *own* it.

That's how you build team efficacy by pushing initiatives forward and grounding them in shared belief.

Promote Communication, Transparency, and Gratitude

As Brené Brown reminds us, "Clear is kind. Unclear is unkind." When change is in motion, transparent communication isn't a luxury—it's a lifeline.

Your team needs to know:
- What's changing
- Why it's changing

- What it means for them
- How they'll be supported

Weekly newsletters. Open-door policies. Feedback loops that actually loop. These aren't "nice-to-haves"—they're culture builders.

Transparency creates trust, which in turn creates safety. Safety creates the space for people to grow—even when it's hard.

Jim Knight reminds us that intentional dialogue matters. When we actively listen, reflect honestly, and respond with empathy, we create schools where people feel *safe to stretch.*

And in the middle of all that stretching, don't underestimate the power of gratitude.

A sticky note on a desk.
A shout-out in a meeting.
A student led thank-you campaign.

These small acts of recognition? They shift the tone of the building. From: "*We're overwhelmed.*" To: "*We're in this together—and we're grateful.*"
Change is hard, but gratitude keeps people grounded in what's good—even when the ground feels shaky.

Leading Through Resistance with Clarity and Compassion

Let's name it: Resistance isn't failure. It's part of the process. People resist change not because they're difficult—but because they're human.

Change disrupts safety, alters identity, and triggers fear of the unknown. Your job as a leader isn't to eliminate resistance. It's to understand it, honor it, and guide people through it with compassion and clarity.

The first step? Listen deeply.

What looks like pushback is often just unspoken fear:
"Will I still be good at this?"
"Will anyone notice if I'm struggling?"

"Do I belong in this new version of the work?"

Give your team permission to be honest. Let them name the fear. Because once something is spoken, it loses its power.

Next, clarify the *why*. People need more than a directive—they need meaning. Not just, "Here's what we're doing," but: "This is why it matters. This is what we believe. This is who benefits."

In moments of tension, return to your anchors: mission, vision, and shared values. These are the handholds when everything else feels uncertain.

Then, celebrate the brave ones, the early adopters, the quiet triers, the ones giving it a shot even when they're nervous. Shine a light on progress. Small wins matter. They multiply.

Finally, support without suffocating. Offer coaching, tools, and encouragement, but give your team space to *own* the change. People commit to what they help create, not what they're micromanaged through.

And above all—be patient.

Real change isn't quick, messy, emotional, or full of detours. But if the purpose is clear and the support is real, transformation happens.

You Were Not Meant to Coast

You were not built to coast through leadership. You were built to grow, stretch, and sometimes struggle.

Change is not a disruption. It's a *doorway*. A doorway to better alignment. To deeper connection. To a school that reflects not just what's required but what's *possible*.

You will face pushback.
You'll question yourself.
You'll wonder if it's worth the weight.

But remember this: Authentic leadership lives in that in-between space—
where vision meets resistance,
where discomfort meets growth,
where doubt meets courage.

That's where your people are. And that's where you're called to lead.

Leadership Soundtrack: From Clarity to Legacy

Track 13: "This Is the Day" – The The

"This is the day / Your life will surely change..."

Numbers don't change lives. Leaders do.

But when you use data to see people more clearly, to ground decisions in shared purpose, and to lead with courage and compassion, change becomes culture, and culture becomes a legacy.

The next chapter invites you to zoom out—to see the systems you've shaped, the impact you've made, and the people who rise because you chose to lead with clarity, heart, and vision.

Because it's never just about a new plan.

It's about the lives transformed because you had the courage to begin.

CHAPTER 14

The Data-Driven Leader

"CHANGE DOESN'T BREAK YOU- IT REVEALS YOU." UNKNOWN

I used to avoid data like it was a math test I hadn't studied for—heart racing, sweaty palms, trying not to make eye contact with the charts on the wall. I'd sit in meetings where spreadsheets were projected onto the screen like a foreign language. There were bar graphs, scatter plots, and acronyms I wasn't sure anyone understood—but everyone nodded anyway. And I nodded, too, hoping no one would ask me a direct question.

I knew the data mattered. I knew it was supposed to help us make decisions, drive instruction, and improve outcomes. But what no one ever really taught me—what no leadership class or textbook explained—was how to take that mountain of information and make it meaningful, how to turn numbers into stories, and how to make data serve people, not the other way around.

For a long time, I believed data belonged to the state, the central office, or the curriculum department. It felt like something that got handed down, something we were supposed to respond to but never interact with. Something we had to "use" because someone said so—not because it felt valuable.

And frankly, I was intimidated. I am a people-first leader. I built trust, culture, and connection. I walked the halls, knew every student's name, and celebrated my staff like family. I didn't want to lose that by becoming overly focused on test scores and charts. I worried that caring too much about data might make me cold. That I'd lose the heart of what I loved about leading.

But here's what I've learned—*data isn't the enemy of heart-centered leadership*. It's the ally. It's one of the most compassionate tools you have.

Data done right doesn't just measure success—it shows you where to focus your love, where to direct your support, and how to reach the kids who need you most. It gives a voice to the quiet students who aren't raising their hands but are trying so hard. It holds a mirror up to our assumptions and helps us see when our best intentions still leave gaps. It tells the story behind the scenes—the one that doesn't show up in behavior charts or classroom participation alone.

But I didn't figure that out overnight. It took trial and error, messy PDs, failed attempts at "data days," and a few brave teachers willing to help me translate all those numbers into human impact. Slowly, I began to see the possibilities.

Eventually, we found a rhythm. We created visuals that made sense. We built systems that centered on student growth, not just final scores. We started talking about trends instead of blaming individuals. And something shifted.

I began to look forward to data meetings—not because they were easy, but because they meant we were *seeing* our kids in more profound ways. We identified wins worth celebrating and needs worth addressing. We made decisions confidently because we had the evidence to back them up.

And that's when I realized something powerful: data done right can feel good. It can empower instead of overwhelm. It can bring clarity instead of confusion. It can be a love language that says, "I see you. I'm paying attention. I care enough to know exactly what you need."

That shift—from fear to fluency—changed everything for me as a leader and is still changing things.

Leading from the Edge—with Data in Hand

VISION MATTERS, BUT WITHOUT DIRECTION, IT'S JUST A DREAM.

When you're leading from the edge—navigating change, disruption, or transformation—you don't have the luxury of guesswork. You can't rely on gut feelings alone. Vision matters, but without direction, it's just a dream. That's where data steps in—not to control you, but to equip you.

Using data regularly helps you take bold steps without blindly leaping into the unknown. It's your map in unfamiliar terrain, your flashlight when the path ahead is dim. It allows you to lead with both courage and clarity.

Without data, leading is like driving at night with no headlights and a fogged-up windshield. You might know the general direction you want to go, but you can't see the curves ahead, the potholes in your path, or the people waiting along the way. You're operating on instinct alone—and while instinct is powerful, it's not precise. You miss things. You drift. You waste time circling back to problems that could have been prevented.

But with data? You gain visibility. Patterns emerge. Struggles become solvable. Strengths become scalable. You're no longer reacting—

you're anticipating. And in leadership, especially on the edge, that changes everything.

Using data doesn't dull your intuition—it sharpens it. It gives your team confidence that their hard work is paying off. It allows you to speak truth to decision-makers, advocate for students with precision, and challenge your own biases along the way.

And when you're leading from the edge—where the footing is uncertain, the pressure is high, and the stakes are personal—data is what gives you a foothold. It's what turns your passion into impact. It's what lets you take risks that are rooted in purpose, not panic.

You don't need to be a statistician. You don't need to love spreadsheets. You just need to care enough to want to know the truth—and be brave enough to act on it.

My Journey with Data: From Intimidation to Inspiration

Early in my principalship, I entered a data meeting and immediately started sweating. There were color-coded spreadsheets everywhere, acronyms flying across the room, and a deep, sinking feeling in my stomach. I felt like an outsider in my school. How was I supposed to lead data conversations when I could barely keep up with the chart on the wall?

But over time, I realized something important: you don't have to be a data expert—you just have to care about what the data is trying to tell you. You must believe that behind every number is a child, and behind every trend is a truth worth uncovering. That was the moment everything changed.

Sidebar: Data Isn't Cold—It's Careful.
One of my teachers once said, "I thought data was just numbers until I realized it was a love language—one that says 'I see you.'" That

changed how we all approached our data days. It wasn't about pressure anymore. It was about purpose.

Once I embraced that mindset, I started turning data into something we could feel, see, and use. We launched initiatives like student data notebooks where kids tracked their growth and set goals.

Kindergarteners pointed at their "walls of fame" and shouted, "That's my goal!"—and they meant it. We celebrated growth like it was a sporting event. Teachers became data detectives, not just data consumers.

And let me tell you—data began to drive the joy, not the fear.

Mirror Moment: What Story Is Your Data Telling?

I often ask my team, "If someone looked only at our data, what story would they think we're telling about our students?" Are we telling a story of equity, growth, and urgency, or one of excuses, overwhelm, and stagnation?

At one of my schools, we told a new story. We used data notebooks, learning goals, and Tier 2/3 intervention tracking to move our 2nd graders from 41% to 63.5% proficient. In 3rd grade, we jumped from 29% to 71%. In 4th, we went from 13% to 55%. And that wasn't by accident. It was by clarity, consistency, and a whole lot of collaboration. That has to start with you, the leader.

And we didn't do it with fancy platforms or expensive programs. We did it by believing that when students know where they are, where they're going, and how to get there—they rise.

Making Data Actionable and Accessible

If data feels like a burden to your staff, chances are it's not being used correctly. The magic happens when you connect the data to your mission and make it something everyone understands and owns.

We started using simple but powerful tools, like:
- "Big 5" Data Walls track key indicators for every student in a visible, ongoing way. Start with 5—it's simply more manageable.
- Cause and Effect Protocols – separating student-centered effect data from adult action-based cause data. How much time are we spending on our priority standards?
- Learning Walks – regular, non-evaluative classroom visits focused on collecting real-time instructional data and lifting best practices.
- Student-Led Conferences – where students explain their growth using their data notebooks and reflections.

Things shifted when data became part of our everyday conversations—not just a quarterly event. Suddenly, everyone had ownership. We weren't chasing numbers anymore. We were pursuing insight, alignment, and action.

Practical Strategy: The 3 A's of Data-Driven Culture

If you want to build a culture where data drives action, here are three simple guiding principles:
1. Accessible – Start with visuals, color coding, and shared systems. Use charts that make sense, goal trackers students can read, and dashboards that celebrate growth—not just gaps.

2. Actionable – Don't gather data unless you plan to use it. Ask: What decisions does this data drive? What interventions does it support? What next steps does it reveal?

3. Affective – Yes, feelings matter. How people feel about data determines how they use it. Help staff feel safe, supported, and successful. Make wins visible. Let growth be the goal.

Help People Fall in Love With the Why

Too often, data is introduced as a compliance tool instead of a clarity tool. If you want your team to love data, you have to frame it as a tool for advocacy. It's not about ranking students. It's about knowing them. It's not about control—it's about empowerment.

I often remind my team that data gives us evidence for celebration and is sometimes a weapon when advocacy is needed. Data is your best backup when facing resource shortages, trying to prove that a child needs services, or demanding professional development in a weak area.

And when you use it to shine a light on what's working, your team begins to see themselves as the story's heroes—not just the targets of accountability.

Vision in One Hand, Data in the Other: Building the Plane While You Fly It

I've always been the kind of leader comfortable "building the plane in the air." I thrive on momentum, creativity, and figuring things out as I go. I believe in innovation. I believe in risk. And I believe in saying, "Let's try it," even before all the pieces are in place.

But I've learned that while you can build the plane mid-flight, you still need an instrument panel, dashboard lights, and information about your height, speed, and direction—because vision without data is just turbulence.

I've come to understand that you don't have to choose between being a visionary and being data-driven. You can be both, and you must be both.

Big thinkers create momentum. They dream of what's possible. They imagine new systems, better outcomes, and radical change. But without data, those dreams stay hypothetical. They never land.

Data-focused leaders, on the other hand, bring structure. They watch for patterns course-correct, and anchor big ideas in real-time feedback and measurable growth.

The sweet spot is in the middle.

When you blend big vision with accurate data, the magic happens. You can dream boldly but also track what's working. You can change course without crashing. You can show your team that your crazy ideas aren't just passionate but purposeful. And the beauty is the more you make data accessible and meaningful, the more your team starts to dream with you. They see the vision not just as "your idea" but as something worth building—together.

So yes, I still build the plane while flying it. But now I've got the gauges, the co-pilot, and a strong tailwind powered by data. And the flight is smoother—and more impactful—than ever before.

Every Student, Every Standard: Turning Data into Action

When I say that data can feel good, this is what I mean.

As mentioned before, one of the most powerful tools we use in our building is something we created ourselves: the Every Student Every Standard (ESES) document. It's more than a spreadsheet. It's a living, breathing map of student progress. It's our compass, our reality check, our rally cry.

Why We Created It

We were swimming in data, yet no one truly felt they owned it. Test scores would roll in once or twice a year, and while everyone nodded along during the meetings, there was an underlying uncertainty—no one knew what to do next. Interventions were happening, but only in pockets. There were good ideas and lots of meetings, but we lacked clarity. We needed a way to see all kids— every day, across every standard. We didn't just want to track completion or participation; we needed something clearly showing us who had mastered what. We had good ideas and plenty of meetings, but we lacked clarity. We didn't just want to track participation—we needed a way to measure mastery, spot gaps, and take real action.

What It Looks Like

The ESES document is organized by the teacher and by standard. Each tab includes:
- Student name
- Date
- Assessment title or type
- Assessment link (if applicable)
- Proficiency level (1–4 scale)
- Proficiency Scale linked for clarity on scoring
- Notes and next steps

The magic lies in the color coding. With just a glance, you can see who is struggling: students in the red zone with a 0 or 1, approaching in yellow (2), and students who have reached proficiency(3) or advanced(4) in green and blue. And this isn't limited to just summative assessments. It captures everything: formative checks, running records, observational notes, exit tickets—you name it.

Teachers input data regularly, and the document updates in real time. It's not just for individual use, either. With tabs organized by teacher and views sorted by standard and student, we can easily spot classroom trends, share what's working, and collaborate with purpose. Our interventions—whether Tier 1, 2, or 3—are now driven by real needs instead of assumptions. We've eliminated duplication, streamlined efforts, and, most importantly, created a system where no child falls through the cracks. Every student matters, and every student grows.

How It Helps

Here's what this tool truly changed: Our PLC conversations got real. No more surface-level data talk or vague summaries. We were naming specific students, pinpointing exact standards, and getting laser-focused on what each kid needed to grow. Our interventions became sharper—no more blanket "extra help" groups. We knew who needed support in that area, and we had a way to measure whether our strategies were working. Teachers began to feel empowered. They weren't overwhelmed by spreadsheets or arbitrary goals—they were tracking real growth, seeing student progress, and taking ownership because the data meant something. It was clear, manageable, and actionable.

As a leader, I got smarter, too. I could confidently walk into meetings, classrooms, or parent conferences—not just tossing around test scores but speaking to specific strengths, gaps, and next steps. But the most impactful change? Our students felt seen. They weren't just "bubble kids" or benchmark labels—individuals with names, faces, stories, and goals. One student saw their color move from red to yellow and whispered, "I'm getting better, right?" Yes. Yes, you are. We celebrated growth at every level and honored effort as much as achievement. When children saw themselves move from a one to a two on the scale, it wasn't just a number. It was momentum. It was belief. It mattered.

It's Not Perfect—But It's Powerful

We still tweak and learn, but the ESES process has become one of the most transformational tools in our data journey. It's accessible, actionable, and aligned. And it proves that data doesn't have to be scary—it can be strategic, student-centered, and joyful.

Mirror Moment:

What story is your school's data telling? Is it clear? Is it hopeful? Is it aligned with your beliefs? You might even print this list, tuck it in your desk drawer, and revisit it before every significant shift.

Practical Strategy: The 3 C's of Transformative Data Use

1. Clarity – Keep the goal in sight. Make expectations, benchmarks, and standards visible and known.
2. Consistency – Collect and reflect routinely. Don't wait for testing windows—use formative data every week.
3. Collaboration – Data lives best in teams. Use it to encourage each other, identify trends, and plan meaningful next steps.

Data That Feels Good

At our first staff meeting about the new data system, one teacher folded their arms and said, "I've been doing it this way for 20 years." I felt the air tighten in the room. That's pre-contemplation. Then someone murmured, "I can see how this might help... I just don't know how we'll fit it in." That's contemplation. Later, one stayed behind and asked for a copy of the rubric. That was preparation. A few weeks in, she was running the data talk herself—action. By spring, she was mentoring others—maintenance.

Let it guide your decisions. Let it ground your leadership. But most of all—let it remind you: data isn't just about the numbers. It's about the names. It's about the growth. It's about love, on purpose.

Leadership Soundtrack: The Heart of Servant Leadership

Track 14: "Good Job" – Alicia Keys

"You're doing a good job / Don't get too down / The world needs you now..."

Servant leadership isn't about fixing everything—it's about showing up, building others, and loving big without losing yourself. This chapter reminded us we can lead with care, clarity, presence, and boundaries. And the truth is—when you lead this way, with a heart that lifts instead of carries, you're already doing a good job. The next chapter leans into the question: what are we leaving behind? Because impact isn't just what we do—it's what lives on in others because we chose to lead from the edge.

CHAPTER 15

Servant Leadership-Empowerment Without Burnout

"Servant leadership isn't about carrying everyone's load-it's about clearing the path for them to carry their own."

Let me start with a confession.

For a long time, I thought servant leadership meant saying "yes" to everything—covering classes, solving everyone's problems, and doing whatever it took to keep people happy. I believed that being selfless meant giving it all away.

Spoiler alert: I ended up exhausted, bitter, and crouched in a storage room, eating a half-smashed granola bar while answering emails on my phone. Ironically, I had nothing left to give—in the name of serving others.

I had misunderstood the assignment.

What Servant Leadership Isn't

Servant leadership isn't about being a martyr in a cute cardigan. It's not people-pleasing disguised as purpose. And it's not about saying "yes" to every ask while ignoring your own health, priorities, or sanity.

If you find yourself doing everyone's job, picking up what others drop, and holding your breath during meetings, hoping no one asks for more—you might not be serving. You might be enabling.

Been there. Learned the hard way.

What Servant Leadership Is

True servant leadership is about empowerment. It lifts others up—not by doing the work for them, but by clearing the path so they can rise. It creates a culture of safety, support, and challenge—a place where people can stretch without fear and lead without asking permission.

It's not about being everything to everyone. It's about helping people believe they already have what it takes.

How Servant Leaders Actually Lead

Servant leadership isn't passive. It's not "whatever you need, I'll do it." It's intentional. Strategic. It's knowing when to step in—and when to step back.

Here's the gut-check I return to when I feel myself slipping into superhero mode:

1. **Empower, don't micromanage**. Trust your team enough to let go of the wheel. If you've trained, supported, and communicated clearly, back up and let them fly. You can't say you believe in people and hover over every detail simultaneously.

2. **Shine the spotlight; don't stand in it.** Celebrate the team wins, the tiny breakthroughs, the quiet rockstars. Leadership isn't about applause—it's about amplification. Pass the mic.

3. **Protect peace; don't praise burnout.** Build a culture that honors boundaries. Notice who's staying late every day and checking in. Normalize leaving on time. Say it with me: exhaustion is not a badge of honor.

Those three checks—trust, credit, and boundaries—have become my inner compass. When I start over-functioning or fixing, I pause and ask: Am I genuinely leading here... or just helping too much?

Mirror Moment: Lead Yourself First

Before you lead others, pause and lead yourself. Ask:
- When did I last feel real joy in leadership—not duty, but delight?
- Where might I be the bottleneck instead of the builder?
- What boundary have I been ignoring that needs honoring this week?

This moment of reflection isn't fluff—it's foundational. You can't pour from a dry cup. So give yourself permission to reset.

Now, choose one slight, intentional shift to make this week:
- Block 30 minutes for deep, uninterrupted planning.
- Say no to a meeting that drains rather than drives.
- Take a walk. Laugh with your team. Shut the laptop before bedtime.
- Delegate that thing you've been holding onto too tightly.

How you lead yourself sets the tone for how your people will lead others.

My Mistakes Along the Way

I once had a teacher—we'll call her "M"—who came to me in tears on a Tuesday afternoon. It wasn't even October, and she was already unraveling. Her classroom was chaotic, her plans and data were empty, and her confidence had disappeared faster than a classroom set of dry-erase markers.

I saw the look in her eyes and thought, This is it. This is my moment to serve. So, I jumped into full superhero mode. I cleared her duties, rearranged her schedule, found her coverage, and even helped plan her lessons. I thought I was being helpful—selfless, even. And for a second, it felt like I'd saved the day. But six weeks later? Same tears. Same overwhelm. Nothing had changed.

Because instead of equipping her, I rescued her. I didn't empower—I enabled. I hadn't coached her forward—I had communicated, You can't do this without me. That realization changed me.

Now, when someone comes to me in a moment of need, I pause and ask one powerful question: "What do you need from me right now—support, space, or strategy?" It's simple. But it shifts the power back where it belongs. Sometimes, they need to vent. Sometimes, they need clarity. And sometimes, they just need to be reminded that they're not alone.

SERVANT LEADERSHIP ISN'T ABOUT FIXING EVERYTHING BUT HELPING PEOPLE FIND THEIR STRENGTH AGAIN.

Servant leadership isn't about fixing everything but helping people find their strength again. That's how we grow resilient staff, not just temporarily relieved ones.

The next time M came to my office, she wasn't crying. She brought a plan. And that's the fruit of doing the deeper work.

Everyone Deserves to Be Led Well

Every person in your building—every teacher, paraprofessional, custodian, secretary, cafeteria worker—deserves to be led well. And let's be clear: being "led well" doesn't mean getting everything you ask for. It doesn't mean never being challenged or living in a bubble of constant praise (although a bit of recognition never hurts).

It means being seen, guided with dignity, consistency, clarity, and respect, and working in a culture where people matter more than checklists and relationships run deeper than roles.

And here's what we don't say out loud nearly enough: **You** deserve to be led well, too.

Sometimes, you are the only one who can give yourself that kind of leadership. You deserve peace—not panic. You deserve systems that don't collapse if you step away. You deserve real joy in your work, not just pressure disguised as purpose.

If your identity is tethered to chaos... if you feel like the whole place will crumble without you... that's not leadership. That's survival. Servant leadership isn't about martyrdom. It's about modeling. When you take care of yourself—when you rest, delegate, protect your boundaries, and trust your people—you show your team what sustainability looks like. You make space for others to grow because you've finally stopped trying to carry it all.

So yes—everyone deserves to be led well. And that starts with you.

Authentic Servant Leadership Starts with the Real You

The best leaders I've ever known weren't the flashiest or the loudest. They weren't the ones with color-coded agendas or the slickest staff emails. They were the ones who showed up—real, grounded, and unapologetically human. They didn't need to be the smartest in the room because they were the most present.

That's when it clicked: leadership isn't about performing. It's about connecting. And people don't follow perfection—they follow authenticity.

For a long time, I thought being the leader meant always being "on"—buttoned up, composed, and emotionally bulletproof. But some of the most transformational moments in my leadership didn't come from having the correct answers. They came from being honest enough to say, "I don't know, but I'll figure it out with you."

Not reckless. Not unfiltered. Just honest.

I stopped trying to lead like a polished version of myself and started leading like me—messy, growing, faith-driven, coffee-fueled me. And something incredible happened. My team leaned in. They trusted me more, not because I had it all together, but because I didn't pretend to. Because I was with them—not above them.

That's what servant leadership really looks like. It's not about being the strongest in the room—it's about being the truest.

When you show up as your whole self, you give others permission to do the same. And that creates something powerful: a culture where people don't just comply—they commit because they feel safe. Because they feel seen.

Servant Leadership Myths—Busted

Let's name the lies. The ones I believed. The ones you might still be carrying.

I used to think saying yes to everything made me supportive, that giving people what they wanted—right away—meant I was doing leadership right, that avoiding hard conversations kept the peace, and that solving every problem made me a hero.

Spoiler alert: it didn't. It made me tired. Resentful. And slowly, it chipped away at my capacity to lead well.

Here's what I've learned:

Myth #1: Saying yes to everything is the servant thing to do. Nope. It's the shortcut to burnout. Healthy servant leadership has boundaries. Saying no—with clarity and compassion—isn't a failure to serve. It's a refusal to sacrifice your mission for short-term comfort.

Myth #2: It's your job to fix everything. Not even close. When you jump in too fast with the solution, you rob people of the chance to build their own skills and confidence. Supporting someone doesn't mean solving for them—it means walking alongside them, asking the right questions, and letting them stretch.

Myth #3: Avoiding conflict keeps the team happy. It doesn't. It just buries the problems deeper. What looks like harmony on the surface often hides dysfunction underneath. Servant leadership doesn't shy away from the tough stuff. It leans in—with kindness, yes—but also with truth.

If you've ever caught yourself over-functioning, avoiding friction, or stretching yourself to the breaking point in the name of being "nice"—you're not alone. I've been there. But growth lives in the undoing. In the unlearning.

Servant leadership is not about being everything to everyone. It's about helping people rise by leading with wisdom, boundaries, and belief. That's where the real impact lives.

Empowerment: The Real Fruit

Here's the truth they don't tell you when you first step into leadership: when you commit to servant leadership—not the performative kind, but the deep, steady, heart-level kind—the transformation is undeniable.

I've seen it. I've lived it. And I can tell you this: empowerment isn't just a buzzword. It's the quiet, steady fire that changes everything.

I think of one staff member who, early on, couldn't take a step without checking with me first. I used to think that meant I was helpful—available, supportive, always on. But I realized I was holding her back. So I backed off. I allowed her to lead a PD, test new strategies, and make mistakes without micromanagement. And guess what? She didn't just grow—she flew. Today, she's one of the most trusted instructional voices in our building. Not because I molded her—but because I moved out of the way.

Then came a moment I'll never forget. A teacher walked into my office looking for directions. Old me would've launched into the solution in under thirty seconds. But instead, I paused and asked, "What do you think we should do?"

She blinked. Thought. Spoke slowly. And in that moment, you could see her confidence clicking into place. That one question—one moment of belief—set something in motion. She didn't just take ownership of the problem. She started leading from it.

That's the fruit of servant leadership. It's not about creating followers who wait for directions—it's about raising up leaders who own the mission.

Empowerment doesn't mean constant hand-holding. It looks like:
- Trust in action.
- Backing someone's play, even when it's imperfect.

- Asking more questions than you answer.
- Creating space for people to rise—and being okay with the mess that comes with growth.

Servant leadership done well doesn't create dependence. It grows boldness. Ownership. Courage. And let me tell you—watching someone rise to their potential because you believed in them? That's one of the greatest joys of leadership. It's the adult version of the classroom lightbulb moment. That's my why.

Practical Strategy: The "Support-Stretch-Celebrate" Framework

Servant leadership doesn't mean doing it all. It means walking alongside your people with clarity, care, and the courage to challenge them when needed. This simple three-part framework became a game-changer for me—and it can guide your everyday leadership moves with intentionality and heart.

1. Support: Meet the Need Without Taking Over

When someone shows up in your office overwhelmed or in tears, start with one powerful question: "What do you need from me—support, space, or strategy?" That one question has saved me from over-functioning more times than I can count. Sometimes, they need to vent; sometimes, they need a tool; and sometimes, they need permission to breathe. Asking helps you respond with intention—not assumption.

Do: Offer presence, not just solutions.
Don't: Jump in to fix it unless invited.

2. Stretch: Grow Capacity, Not Dependency

Challenge your people with care. Give them leadership moments. Ask for their plan before offering yours. One of my favorite go-to phrases: "What's your first step?" It reminds you believe in their instincts, growth, and ability to rise. I tell new hires they'll get support, fun, and a culture that cares deeply. But I won't promise comfort—because growth lives outside of it. That's not pressure—it's belief.

Do: Coach with curiosity.
Don't: Assume they can't handle the hard stuff.

3. Celebrate: Spotlight the Growth, Not Just the Outcome

Recognition builds culture. Cheer for results—but also courage, risk, and effort. Use shoutouts, hallway celebrations, handwritten notes, or surprise awards. Celebrate loudly, publicly, and often.

Do: Praise progress consistently and sincerely.
Don't: Wait for perfection.

When you lead with Support, Stretch, and Celebration, your people don't just survive the year—they rise. And you don't burn out trying to carry everyone. You walk beside them, step for step, building a culture strong enough to outlast the hardest days.

Lead Well, Love Big, and Let Go of the Rest

Servant leadership, at its heart, is simple. It's not always easy—but simple.

Lead with integrity, love with intention, and let go of anything that makes leadership about control, perfection, or performance.

That means releasing the ego that whispers you must have all the answers. Releasing the fear that says if you don't do it, no one will. Releasing the habits that turn you into the fixer instead of the builder.

You were never meant to be the hero of everyone's story.

You were meant to be the guide—the steady hand, the kind truth-teller, the leader who makes room for others to rise.

Let go of the need to carry it all. Let go of the myth that servant leadership means sacrificing yourself for everyone else's needs. Let go of the version of you that leads from depletion and step into the one that leads from strength—real, rooted, human strength.

Lead well—with clarity, courage, and care.

Love big—with boundaries, belief, and boldness.

And let go of the rest. Because the best leaders don't do it all—they make sure no one has to do it alone.

Leadership Soundtrack: From Serving Adults to Centering Kids

Track 15: "Do Something" – Matthew West

"I woke up this morning / Saw a world full of trouble now... / I just couldn't bear the thought of people living in poverty... / And I said, 'God, why don't You do something?' / He said, 'I did—I created you.'"

Servant leadership isn't about doing it all—it's about doing the next right thing with courage, purpose, and people in mind.

It's seeing a need and stepping in—not out of obligation, but out of conviction. It's building systems that empower others, noticing what's broken, and choosing to be the one who does something about it.

That "something" might be advocating for your team, creating space for new voices, or drawing boundaries that protect your energy and theirs. It might mean saying yes to mentoring, no to burnout, and always, always yes to the kids.

Because while we serve adults with empathy and care, our deepest why is still sitting in classrooms, waiting to be seen.

Chapter 16 brings the focus back to them—the kids who don't need a superhero, just someone who shows up.

Someone who listens.

Someone who leads with them in mind.

Because the real impact? It's not in the title.

It's in what you choose to do next.

The "Kids First" Philosophy

"EVERY CHILD YOU PASS IN THE HALL HAS A STORY THAT
NEEDS TO BE HEARD."

Let me tell you about K.

He was a second grader with a spark that could light up a room—or
set it on fire, depending on the day. His file was three inches thick,
packed with documentation from a childhood full of transitions,
trauma, and too many school changes. Long before he ever walked
into our building, his reputation arrived first.

Teachers braced themselves. Honestly? So did I.

Then, one morning, I found him sitting cross-legged in the hallway
outside my office. Head down. Silent tears slid down his cheeks. He
wasn't in trouble. No one had sent him. He just showed up.

So I did, too.

I sat down beside him on that cold tile floor. No clipboard. No expectations. Just presence. After a few quiet moments, I asked softly, "What's going on?"

He didn't look up. Wiped his face with the sleeve of his hoodie. Then whispered, "You're not giving up on me... are you?"

Something inside me cracked wide open.

I shook my head. "Nope. Sorry, buddy," I said. "You can do hard things. And you are good."

Because here's what I believe to my core: there are no "bad kids." Just kids with hurt. Kids make hard choices because they haven't yet been given the tools to make better ones. K didn't think he'd made bad choices—he believed he was bad. Flawed. Unlovable.

But I've never met a kid beyond hope. Not one.

That day, I made him a promise. I told him I wasn't going anywhere. I'd keep showing up, listening, and believing in him—even when he didn't believe in himself.
I
 even joked, "Are you getting in trouble just to come hang out in my office?"

He cracked a sheepish grin. "Maybe," he said.

Stinker.

Kids Are the Mission.

We spend so much time discussing data points, pacing guides, and academic benchmarks. And yes, those things matter. But they are not the mission.

Kids are.

Sometimes, the most powerful thing we can offer isn't a curriculum or a consequence—it's our presence. It's being seen, heard, and valued beyond behavior. It's sitting on a hallway floor and saying, "You matter," when everything in a child's life might tell them otherwise.

When we consistently show up for kids like K—even when it's messy—we don't change their story.

We change ours.

Mirror Moment: Who needs to be seen?

Think about your own "K." That student, staff member, or family who pushes your buttons or pulls your energy might not be testing your patience—they might be testing whether you'll stay.

- Have you ever misread a cry for connection as a behavior to correct?
- What would it look like to respond with presence instead of punishment?
- When's the last time you told someone, "I see you—and I'm not giving up"?

Pause here. Let it settle. Because leadership isn't just about what you do—it's about how you see.

When in Doubt, Go to the Kids

In the swirl of leadership—deadlines, directives, logistics—losing your center is easy. We chase initiatives, manage adults, and put out fires.

But when the overwhelm rises or the clarity fades, here's what I've learned: Go be with the kids.

Walk through the cafeteria. Pop into a kindergarten class. Listen to a student read. Eat lunch beside the kid who's been shut down lately. Let them remind you why you started.
Because they always do.

That's the heart of the "Kids First" philosophy: Every decision, every system, every strategy should lead us back to them. Not just the easy kids. Not just the high achievers. Every. Single. Child.

Practical Strategy: The Kids First Filter

One of the simplest, most transformative tools I've ever used as a leader isn't a program or a product. It's a mindset filter I use to make every decision—a gut check I call the Kids First Filter.

> **EVERY DECISION, EVERY SYSTEM, EVERY STRATEGY SHOULD LEAD US BACK TO THEM.**

When facing a choice, big or small, ask yourself:
- Does this serve students or systems?
- Will this protect or promote learning, safety, or belonging for kids?
- If students watched this decision unfold, would they feel seen, supported, or dismissed?

These questions may seem simple, but consistently applying them shifts everything—from how you design policies to how you handle discipline, schedule meetings, or plan PD.

We had a student—Emily—who visited the nurse six times in one week. She had headaches and stomach aches and was "just not feeling right." The instinct was to call home, redirect her, or push her back to class. But I paused. I ran it through the filter.

- Serve students or systems? Systems.
- Promote belonging? No.
- Would she feel seen? Definitely not.

So I invited her to lunch. We played Uno. We didn't dig deep. We just connected. The nurse visits stopped. Attendance improved. Her reading scores went up. Because the issue wasn't medical—it was emotional. She didn't need a nurse. She needed a connection.

So, I ask you: Will you be the kind of leader who fights for systems or the one who fights for students? Are you willing to be different, even when it's not convenient? Leadership doesn't need more noise. It needs more clarity. And that clarity starts and ends with kids.

Kids Will Tell Your Leadership Story

One day—long after your name is off the door and someone else sits in your chair—the kids you served will carry your story.

Not the accolades.
Not the spreadsheets.
But the way you made them feel.

They'll remember if you listened.
If you saw them.
If you showed up with both policies and heart.

And that—that's legacy.

I think about it often: What will they say about me when I'm not in the room anymore?

If they say, "*She knew my name. She believed in me. She made me feel safe,*" I'll know I led well.

Mirror Moment: What's One Decision You Made This Year That Put Kids First?

Think back. What was a hard decision you made that prioritized student growth, joy, or safety—even when it cost you comfort, popularity, or convenience?

What might shift if *every* decision had to pass through that same lens?

Practical Strategy: Write Your Leadership Legacy Statement

You don't need a five-year plan to lead with purpose.
You just need a clear compass.

Try this: Imagine a former student writing you a letter five years ago. What do they say? How did you make them feel?

Now, write a one-paragraph legacy statement. Something like:

I want to be the leader who sees the kid behind the chaos, builds systems that serve real human beings and leads so that every child—especially the overlooked ones—feels seen, heard, and safe.

Print it. Post it. Let it guide you.

Be Willing to Lead Differently

That one figure stepping off the main path while everyone else keeps marching?

That's you.

That's what real leadership looks like—not climbing higher just for the title but stepping aside to serve more honestly. Boldly. Authentically.

You don't need a polished plan. You just need a clear purpose—and courage that's real. And when you lead with kids at the center—always—you'll never lose your way.

Leadership Soundtrack: Legacy in Motion

Track 16: "Lean On Me" – Bill Withers

"You just call on me, brother, when you need a hand..."
Putting kids first isn't a strategy—it's a standard. A compass. A way of leading that, when lived long enough, lifts everyone around you.

In the final chapter, we shift our gaze beyond the present and into the ripple effect. Legacy doesn't live in job titles—it lives in the lives we've changed and the leaders we've raised.

The edge becomes a beginning—for someone else.

That's when you know you've made your mark.

CHAPTER 17

Growing New Leaders

"A LEADER CREATES MORE LEADERS, NOT MORE FOLLOWERS."- TOM PETERS

Someone Believed in Me (Before I Did)

I was in my third year of teaching—two babies under two, a 50-minute commute, and a heart full of love for my tiny rural school. But it was time for a change. I had just submitted my resignation when the superintendent started walking across the playground toward me.

Cue internal panic: *What had I done?*

But instead of frustration, he simply said, "I saw your resignation. I'm sad to see you go."

That alone would've meant the world. It was gracious. Kind. Respectful. But then he followed it up with something that floored me.

"Well," he said, "just be sure to come see me when you become a principal."

I blinked. Laughed. Shook my head. "Oh no," I said. "Not me! I'm getting my master's in curriculum and instruction. I'm going to teach forever."

He smiled, nodded, and repeated—calmly, like it was already decided: "Okay. Well, come see me when you're a principal."

I thought he was crazy.

But you know what? He was the first person to name leadership in me—before I ever saw it myself. And it stuck. His belief planted a seed. And sure enough, that seed grew.

I'm still unsure whether to thank or scold him for what he got me into (ha!)—but I'll never forget that moment because someone saw something in me and said it out loud. Thank you, Mr. Wilson.

Legacy Isn't a Title—It's a Ripple

When I think about legacy, I don't picture plaques or trophies. I don't think about accolades, awards, or titles. I think about people.

I think about the paraprofessional who grew into a confident, compassionate teacher—and now coaches others. I think about the new hire who used to sit quietly in staff meetings but now mentors first-year teachers with boldness and grace.

I think about a former student who returned to student-teach in the same classrooms that shaped them.

That's what authentic leadership does. It multiplies itself. It doesn't hoard knowledge. It doesn't guard the spotlight. It doesn't fear being replaced.

It builds. It invites. It makes room. It says, "Come with me. Let's do this together."

But here's the truth about legacy: You don't build it alone.

The best teams aren't carbon copies of the leader. They're not made up of people who always agree or think alike. The best teams are built with purpose. They fill your gaps. They challenge your blind spots. They sharpen your thinking—but share your vision.

They show up when the work is messy, the decisions are complicated, and the path is uphill. These are the people you fight beside—for kids, for culture, and for the kind of impact that outlasts you.

When Mrs. Osborne, our school counselor, and dear friend, passed away unexpectedly, it wrecked us. You might remember her from earlier in this book—her presence, laughter, and legacy woven into every hallway she walked. She was empathy and truth, joy and presence. Her legacy wasn't defined by how long she lived but by how deeply she loved.

And she didn't wait to build that legacy *later*. She lived in a way that made it inevitable.

After she passed, one of our teachers saved a small plant from her office and nurtured it back to life. When I left that building after a decade of joyful, chaotic, unforgettable seasons, she gifted me a piece of that plant.

She handed it to me, saying, "You carry on the legacy now. We've got it from here."

That plant sits in my office today—miraculously still alive—and I don't just see green leaves every time I look at it.

I see possibility.
I see heart.

I see a legacy rooted in kindness, service, and purpose.

Legacy isn't about what you leave behind. It's about how you lead while you're still here. It's built in people—not programs. In moments—not monuments. And if you're doing it right? You're not just leaving something behind—you're launching something forward.

Legacy Isn't Left—It's Lived

We talk a lot about *leaving* a legacy—as if it's something we pack up and pass on when we retire. But I've learned legacy isn't what you leave behind. It's how you *live* right now.

Legacy is in the quiet, ordinary moments that don't make the meeting minutes. It's celebrating a new teacher's first bulletin board like the Sistine Chapel. It's in sitting at a basketball game on a Tuesday night just because you know your presence will matter.

It's in how you empower someone to lead—even when they don't feel ready. It's in how you respond when the moment is hard and all eyes are on you. It's in every decision you make that tells your team, *This is who we are. This is how we do things here.*

For me, it's that little green plant from Mrs. Osborne's office—the one I carry with me still. Not because it's fancy or perfect (trust me, it's not), but because it reminds me that leadership is growth passed from one heart to the next.

Legacy isn't someday.
It's **today.**
It's what you model in the hallway, in the meeting, in the email, in the whisper behind closed doors.

It's the courage you show in the face of conflict.
The grace you extend when someone falls short.

Sometimes leadership is as simple and profound as lifting someone's eyes when they've forgotten who they are. That's the kind of presence that leaves a lasting imprint.

So consider this:

- What does your daily leadership communicate about what you truly believe?
- How do people feel after spending time at a table you lead?
- And in this very moment, what kind of culture are you shaping—through your words, your actions, and your presence?

You don't build a legacy with a binder or a five-year plan. You build it by showing up when no one's clapping, the pressure is on, and it would be easier to walk away.

LEGACY ISN'T LEFT. IT'S LIVED.

Legacy isn't left. It's *lived.*

Hiring for Legacy, Not Just a Vacancy

One of the most powerful ways to grow new leaders is through how we hire—not just filling a vacancy but planting seeds. I've always said: *If it's not good enough for my own kids, it's not good enough for anyone's.* That's the lens I use for every hiring decision, classroom setup, policy, and program.

Would I want this person in front of my child?
Would I feel confident dropping off my babies here each morning?

We keep looking if the answer is anything less than a solid yes.

Building a school culture where I'd proudly enroll my own kids means creating a place that is safe, joyful, rigorous, and rooted in love. And that starts with the people we bring through the door.

When I interview someone, I'm not just checking for credentials. I'm listening for heart. I want to know if they are here for the work or the calling.

Do they light up when they talk about kids? Do they speak about growth with curiosity, not ego? Do they reflect, ask meaningful questions, and lean into the challenge—not away from it?

I've learned this the hard way: You can teach the curriculum. You can coach instructional strategy. But you can't fake heart. You can't coach someone to care.

At our school, we've built a reputation for being a place where people grow—because we expect them to. We celebrate risk-taking. We value reflection. We invest in coaching. We believe in people before they believe in themselves sometimes—and that belief starts before Day One.

If we want to build a leadership pipeline, we can't just hire for the current need. We have to hire with tomorrow in mind. Look for leadership instincts—even if they're buried. Water that potential. Coach it. Challenge it. Cheer for it.

And don't just wait for the "right" people to apply. Attract them. Let your culture speak for itself. Let your messaging, energy, and presence say: *This is where people grow. This is where legacies begin.*

Hiring for Leadership Potential

I don't just hire for résumés—I hire for ripple effects. When I'm sitting across from a candidate, I'm thinking beyond their classroom. I'm thinking about the future of our school.

Will this person challenge us to be better? Will they lift others? Will they lead from wherever they are—even without a title?

Because I'm not just hiring teachers, I'm building a team of future leaders—a team that thinks differently, loves boldly, and keeps kids at the center. And hiring like that takes courage, clarity, and the willingness to choose *potential over polish*.

Every hire is a chance to shape your culture. Every interview is a step toward legacy. Before I say yes to a candidate, I ask our team:

- Do they align with our mission—or just check the boxes on the job description?
- Are they here for the kids—or just for the commute?
- Do they light up when they talk about student growth and equity?
- Do they ask curious, meaningful questions about our culture?
- Can I picture them coaching others one day—or receiving coaching with grace?
- Do they handle scenario questions with empathy and clarity?
- Would I want them to influence the next generation of teachers and students?
- And maybe most importantly... will they sharpen me or us?

Because the best hires won't just follow—they'll help you grow. Let's be real: you can teach someone how to use a pacing guide. You can walk them through your curriculum platform. But you can't teach someone to be a good human. You can't train heart.

That's why I watch carefully—not just for polished answers, but for the *moments in between*. The way they speak about kids. The stories they tell. The glimmers of passion they didn't rehearse.

You're not just building a staff when you hire for leadership potential. You're building a future. You're planting seeds that will grow long after you're gone.

Interview Scenarios: Finding Future Leaders

When I'm hiring, I want more than surface answers. These real-life scenarios help uncover how someone thinks, leads, and responds when it counts. Below are simplified versions of my go-to questions, designed to spotlight empathy, collaboration, and a leadership mindset.

Scenario 1: The Disruptive Student
A student with frequent behavior challenges acts out during your lesson—refusing to work and distracting others. What do you do? **What to listen for:** Empathy, de-escalation, classroom management, understanding of trauma-informed practices.
Scenario 2: The Team Conflict
Your grade-level team disagrees on how to teach a major unit. Tension is rising, and time is short. What's your next step? **What to listen for:** Willingness to collaborate, leadership mindset, and ability to respectfully navigate hard conversations.
Scenario 3: The Upset Parent
A parent emails saying you're not meeting their child's needs. How do you respond? **What to listen for:** Emotional intelligence, professionalism under pressure, commitment to problem-solving, and ability to build trust with families.
Scenario 4: The Struggling Colleague
You notice a teammate falling behind—overwhelmed, stressed, and distant. How do you support them? **What to listen for:** Awareness, care, leadership potential, and a team-first mindset.

Bonus Question: What Does Legacy Leadership Mean to You?

The ideal answer is: "Legacy means making a difference that lasts. It's about helping others grow—not being the center but the spark."

Mirror Moment: When They Become You

There's a moment in leadership—quiet, almost sneaky—when you realize someone is leading the way you lead. You hear your words in their voice. You notice your tone mirrored in their coaching. You see your beliefs reflected in how they support others.
And it hits you: They were watching. They were learning from *you*.

That's the beautiful, humbling, and sometimes terrifying part of growing leaders. Your habits become their blueprint, your presence becomes their model, and your blind spots can become theirs, too.

So pause and ask yourself:
- Who on my team is quietly absorbing how I lead?
- What am I unintentionally modeling in my tough moments?
- Am I leading the way I'd want them to lead someday?

Mentorship doesn't always come with a title. Sometimes, it's a passing comment, a side-by-side moment, or a small act of belief that changes everything.

Practical Strategy: Designing a Leadership Pipeline That Works

Leadership development doesn't happen by accident. If you want to grow leaders within your school, you need a system. Here's how to build one—right where you are:

1. Spot It Early: Look for natural leaders—the ones who step up without being asked, support their teammates, or bring calm in a crisis.

2. Name It Out Loud: Tell them what you see. "You handled that like a leader." These words plant potent seeds of belief.

3. Create Micro-Moments to Lead: Give them something small with meaning: lead a PLC, facilitate a team meeting, support a new hire, or plan part of PD.

4. Coach Alongside, Not Above: Let them shadow you. Debrief tough decisions. Offer feedback. Let them wrestle with leadership in real-time.

5. Normalize the Messy Middle Share your growth process—especially your mistakes. Let them see that leadership is learned, not gifted. Be real.

6. Celebrate Leadership in Action: Highlight when someone leads well—especially without a title. Recognition fuels confidence.

7. Build a Ladder, not a Cliff: Don't just inspire—equip. Make sure they know how to move from teacher-leader to official leadership if they choose to. Show them the path, then walk it with them.

Legacy Isn't a Checklist—It's a Culture

Here's what I know for sure: you are not just shaping classrooms—you're shaping futures. Every decision you make, moment of belief you extend, and courageous choice you model is leadership. That's legacy.

And it doesn't live in end-of-year awards or retirement speeches. It lives in the culture you build, the leaders you grow, and how people feel because you were in the room. You don't grow new leaders by micromanaging. You grow them by believing in them. You don't build a legacy by checking boxes. You build it by asking:

- Who needs a voice at this table?

- What barriers can I remove so someone else can rise?
- How do I create space—not just for greatness, but for growth?

The truth is that people don't leave schools—they leave cultures. They leave leadership that makes them feel small. They leave environments where taking the initiative is punished, not praised.

But people stay when they feel seen. They grow when risk is safe, and feedback is honest. They lead when someone invites them forward, not just upward.

If you want to grow new leaders, stop guarding the gate. Hold it open. Wave them in. Then, walk beside them as they build something that might outlast you.

That's not weakness—it's wisdom. That's not losing your role—it's multiplying your reach. That's how legacy moves from a name on the door to a movement that lives on long after you leave the building.

Leadership Soundtrack

Track 17: "For Good" – Wicked the Musical

"Because I knew you, I have been changed for good."

This song doesn't just mark a moment—it is the moment—the one where accolades don't measure your leadership legacy but the lives forever altered by your presence.

The next chapter brings it full circle—your why, rhythm, and *leadership soundtrack.*

Legacy Side Note: For Mrs. Osborne

Melissa,

There's not a day in this work when I don't think of you. Your laughter still echoes in my mind, your warmth still lives in every hallway you once walked, and your impact—your legacy—shows up in the most unexpected and beautiful ways.

You taught me so much, whether you knew it or not. You taught me never to wait or hesitate to tell people when they are essential to me, how to lead with empathy, show up with heart, and never underestimate the power of simply being present for people. You didn't just do your job—the job you weren't sure you could do—you loved people through theirs. You saw kids that others might have missed. You lifted staff who were barely hanging on. You gave generously, quietly, and consistently. You listened. You laughed. You were a safe place for all of us.

That plant from your office? It still grows in mine. Every leaf reminds me that legacies don't always roar—sometimes, they grow quietly, steadily, and beautifully in the lives of others. Your legacy lives in me. It lives in this work. And it lives in the thousands of moments you made brighter just by being there.

I hope you know, from way up there, how much you mattered and how much you still do. This chapter, this book, and much of this journey are for you. Thank you for showing us how to lead well and love big.

You are with us. Still. Always. 🤍

CHAPTER 18

The Soundtrack of Your Legacy

"Life's not about waiting for the storm to pass...it's about learning to dance in the rain." — Vivian Greene

When the Music Hits Different

Let me tell you about when *Get Back Up Again* became more than a song—it became my oxygen.

I had fallen—hard. Not metaphorically. Not professionally. Physically. Emotionally. Spiritually. And it wasn't the first time. But somehow, I heard the beat in those quiet, cracked, and chaotic moments. The message. The call.

I wasn't done. And neither are you.

Leadership at the edge demands a soundtrack. Something that lifts you when you feel like staying down. Something that reminds you who you are when everything around you tells you otherwise.

For me, the anthem has changed over the years—*Overcomer,*

Rescue, Rise Up—each one narrating a chapter of my life. Yours will be different—and it should be. The song you need is the one that brings you back to your why.

 ## Mirror Moment: What's on Your Playlist?

Think back. What's the song that's picked you up off the floor? What lyrics have whispered *"You can"* when everything else screamed "You can't"? What quote, scripture, or voice repeats in your soul when the noise gets loud?

Now—claim it.

That's your anthem. Your reset button. Your reminder.

Oxygen First

That cliché about putting on your oxygen mask first?
Turns out—it's not a suggestion. It's survival.

For the longest time, I thought I wouldn't need to if I ensured everyone else could breathe. I thought I could carry everyone. Spoiler: you can't.

You have to breathe.
You have to pause.
You have to give yourself what you so willingly give to others.

And that includes grace.

The Power of Naming and Reflection

One of the best tools I've found for staying grounded is simply *naming* what I'm experiencing:

- "This is my first time leading through this kind of crisis."

- "This is a season of burnout."
- "This feels unfamiliar, and I'm scared."

Naming your experience doesn't make you weak.
It makes you aware. And awareness breeds growth.
Try asking yourself:

- What's working well that I've forgotten to celebrate?
- What challenge keeps showing up—and why?
- What system might be creating the very behavior I'm trying to change?

Systems Build Culture

If you want to understand your school's culture, don't look at the mission statement—look at your systems.

Where do people park? That's a system.
How do you handle conflict? That's a system.
How are decisions made? What gets celebrated? What gets ignored?
Systems shape behavior. Behavior shapes culture.

So, do you want to shift culture?
Start with the systems.

It's not sexy. But it's transformational.

Final Thoughts: What's Your Soundtrack?

Let this chapter be your permission slip:

To laugh.
To cry.
To fall and get back up—again and again.

You're not behind.

You're becoming.

And the moment you start believing in the leader you are *becoming?*
Everything changes.

What Defines You

The title you hold isn't what defines you.
Not the district you work in.
Not the role. Not the signature at the bottom of your emails.

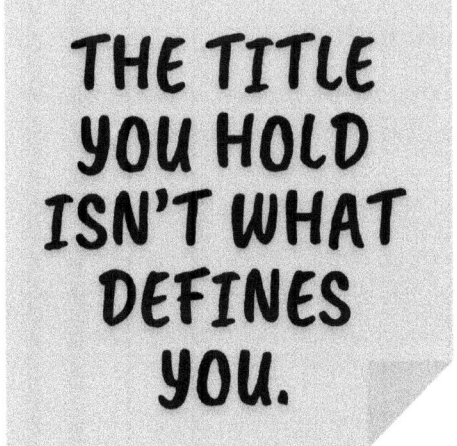

What defines you are your values. Your faith. Your integrity.
If you don't name them, the world will name them for you.

And that's how leaders lose themselves.

You must know what matters so deeply that when the noise comes
(and it will), you don't bend into someone else. You don't become a
copy. You are not alone in this work. But you must stay anchored in
the truth of who you are and who you were made to be.

You remain you.

And About That Faith...

I don't know where you land spiritually—but for me?
There is no way I would have made it through any of this without God.
Not once.
I've stopped praying for comfort.
Now, I pray for clarity.
(Okay... I still pray for patience, too. And I still get "opportunities" to practice it—usually in the form of chaos, tornadoes, or very chatty kindergarteners.)
God knows I'm stubborn, so He sends the lesson loud.
And I'm learning—finally—that rest isn't weakness.
It's wisdom.

Your Legacy Track

You are capable.
You are resilient.
You arc wircd for impact.
So keep dancing in the storm.
Keep singing even when your voice shakes.
Keep showing up when it would be easier to shrink back.
And always—always—lead from the edge.

As your soundtrack plays on—through the chaos, the calm, and every note in between—you realize something: it was never about just leading others. It was always about becoming a leader who shows up fully, loves deeply, and leaves the work better than you found it. And now, as we step into this final reflection, we turn the volume down just enough to hear what mattered most all along—your legacy.

Leadership Soundtrack:

Track 18: "Unwritten" – Natasha Bedingfield

As we reach the final chapter, it's tempting to tie it all up with a bow. But legacy doesn't live in neat conclusions—it lives in the ripple effects of your choices, your presence, your courage. You don't have to have it all figured out. You just have to show up and write the next right line. Like Natasha Bedingfield sings in *"Unwritten," "Live your life with arms* wide open. Today is where your book begins—the rest is still unwritten." What comes next is up to you. And that's exactly where the magic lives.

Epilogue: Stay the Course-Even If You Drew It Yourself

You made it.

Not just to the end of this book—but to the heart of what it means to lead with intention. This is where fear and courage meet, where leadership gets real, raw, and ridiculously beautiful. My hope is that you see it now:

- You were never meant to play it safe.
- You were meant to lead brave on purpose—right where it matters most.
- You were never meant to lead from the center of comfort. You were meant to lead from the edge of what matters most.

If you remember nothing else, remember this:

You are not alone. Not in the overwhelm, the overthinking, or the ocean of responsibility that leadership brings. I've cried in my car. I've questioned my calling. I've drafted resignation letters and applied to every job imaginable (even ones that made no sense). I've failed forward more times than I can count.

What You Carry With You

I hope you walk away from this book with more than ideas—I hope you walk away with intention. From *Lead Anyway* to *The Soundtrack of Your Legacy*, you've been reminded that leadership isn't about perfection. It's about presence, courage, and choosing people—every single time. It's about showing up when it's hard, standing firm when it's blurry, and rising again when you fall.

Here's a walk back through the journey we've taken:

The **Introduction**
Invited you to lead anyway—*even at the edge*—where the risk, growth, and impact live.

Chapter 1
Reminded us that courage begins in chaos. You don't need a perfect plan; you just need to stand up.

Chapter 2
Showed that trust isn't built with titles but with heart. Lead with presence before policy.

Chapter 3
Anchored us in values—your true north when everything else shifts.

Chapter 4
Walked us through the fall—and the rebuild. Resilience isn't fast. It's faithful.

Chapter 5
Taught us that everything else eventually falls apart if you don't lead yourself first.

Then, we turned outward—toward culture.

Chapter 6
Reminded us that culture keeps the ship afloat when a crisis hits.

Chapter 7
Showed how to rebuild a community one relationship, routine, and expectation at a time.

Chapter 8
Revealed that gratitude isn't fluff—it's fuel. It shifts teams and rewires brains.

Chapter 9
Reminded us that joy isn't an accident—it's a strategy. Lead loud. Love big.

And then came trust and the teams that carry it:
Chapter 10

Began with a woman in a parking lot—and the truth that humility is the foundation of community.

Chapter 11
Declared that you're allowed to begin again. And again. Because leadership is human work.

Chapter 12
Taught us to name what's good—because what you name, you nurture.

Chapter 13
Reminded us that change is always hard—but you were built for it.

Chapter 14
Reframed data not as pressure but as purpose. It's not about numbers—but names.

In the final stretch, we redefined what legacy means.

Chapter 15
Called us to real servant leadership, not burnout disguised as service.

Chapter 16
Brought it back to the center: the kids, every decision, every system, every day.

Chapter 17
Invited us to grow new leaders—to multiply the mission, not just maintain it.

Chapter 18
Left us with a soundtrack—a legacy of becoming, rising, and leading with your whole heart.

Now, it's your turn to live it forward.

Your Leadership Soundtrack

Whether your anthem is Overcomer, Get Back Up Again, or a random 90s ballad that no one else understands—it's yours. Let it lift you when you fall, anchor you when you drift, and remind you of your identity when the noise gets too loud.

You're Not Just Building Schools

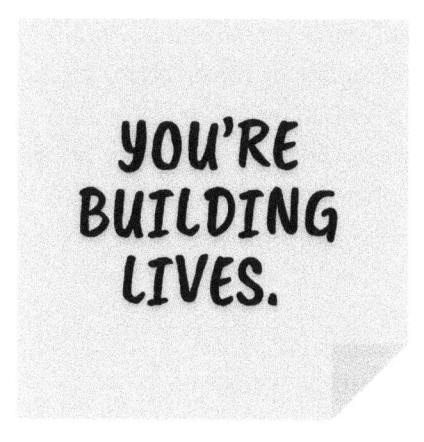

You're building lives. You're not writing lesson plans—you're writing futures. You're not just leading teams—you're shaping legacies. So laugh loudly (especially in front of kids—it throws them off in the best way). Love hard. Show up. Every hallway interaction. Every Post-it. Every hard conversation. It matters more than you know.

And when the path gets blurry?

Lead anyway.
Even if no one else has walked it.
Even if you drew the map in Sharpie.
Especially then.
Because of this edge? This beautiful, unpredictable, faith-soaked edge—is where leaders are made.

Final Mirror Moment: Stay Your Course

So, lead with a clipboard in one hand and a coffee in the other. Wear the silly socks. Cry in the car. Be the one who smiles first. Be the one who stays kind in the chaos. And when it gets heavy (because it will), remember your legacy isn't something you leave behind.

It's something you live—every day.

Stay your course. With courage. With joy. With faith.
Because life is way too short not to love what you do.

And you? You were made for this edge.

So, keep leading with conviction. Keep building with heart. Keep dancing in the storm, even when your shoes are soaked, and the music feels faint. Because somewhere, someone is watching you—learning from you—rising because of you. And one day, long after the emails are gone, and the nameplate is dusted off, your impact will remain, not in programs or policies—but in people. And that's the kind of legacy that never fades. That's what it means to lead from the edge.

Leadership Soundtrack - Epilogue Track:

"Don't Give Up On Me" – Andy Grammar

Leadership isn't about reaching the end of the road—it's about staying the course when the path twists, narrows, or disappears entirely. The title of this book is more than a metaphor; it's a reminder that even on the edge, you can still lead. You can still love. You can still believe. As Andy Grammer sings in *"Don't Give Up On Me,"* *"I'm not giving up, I'm not giving up, giving up, no, not yet."* This isn't the end. It's a reaffirmation. Of who you are. Of why you lead. Of what still matters. Stay the course—even if you drew it yourself.

ABOUT THE AUTHOR

Samatha Hamilton is an award-winning school principal, national education consultant, and unapologetically real leader who believes schools should be where joy and purpose collide. With more than two decades of experience in early childhood education and school leadership, she's known for turning vision into action—and heart into strategy.

Born in Joplin, Missouri and raised by two educators, Samantha was "teaching" both real and imaginary students by the age of five. That early calling grew into a career defined by faith, humor, and an unshakable belief in relationships over rules. Whether she's leading a building, coaching new leaders, or navigating chaos with compassion, Samantha brings presence, grit, and just enough glitter to shift the atmosphere.

She has served in both public and charter schools, taught multiple grades, and led school communities through tornadoes, transitions, staffing crises, and deep cultural transformation. Her leadership philosophy is simple: people first, always. Her impact? Anything but simple.

Beyond the school walls, Samantha mentors aspiring leaders, develops curriculum, and trains educators across the country on topics like school culture, data-driven decision-making, resilience, and servant leadership (minus the burnout). She is a doctoral candidate in Organizational Leadership and a proud wife, mom of three, and Christmas-loving, data-driven chaos coordinator who brings both the fun and the focus to everything she leads.

Study Group Call to Action: Lead Loud. Reflect Deeper.

This book wasn't meant to sit on a shelf—it was meant to spark conversations. Real ones. With laughter, vulnerability, hard questions, and maybe a few "me too" moments.

If you're reading this with a leadership team, a book club, or just a few trusted colleagues, here's your challenge:

- Don't just read—**respond.**
- Don't just agree—act.
- Don't just discuss the ideas—**decide** what they'll look like in your school.

Start your group with three things:

- A notebook or digital journal.
- An open heart.
- A willingness to lead from the edge.

Brave on Purpose Study Group Guide

You can use this as a week-by-week or chapter-by-chapter companion.

Chapter 1 – The Mindset of a Courageous Leader
What edge are you currently leading from?
- What internal narrative do you need to rewrite as a leader?
- How can you replace self-doubt with intentional courage this week?

Chapter 2 – Leading with Heart
Are you leading with your whole self?
- How does empathy show up in your leadership?
- When did your team last see your heart—not just your plan?

Chapter 3 – Know Who You Are: Leading With Core Values
What's your leadership core?
- What are your top three core values right now?
- Where are you aligned—and where are you drifting?

Chapter 4 – From Breaking Point to Breakthrough
What's your rebuild story?
- Where have you led from a place of pain or exhaustion?
- What did you learn about yourself in that season?

Chapter 5 – Leading Yourself First

What rhythms help you lead from wholeness?

- How are you caring for your leadership health?
- What boundary do you need to protect this month?

Chapter 6 – Culture Over Crisis

What sustains your school when everything else shakes?

- What daily practices hold your culture together?
- How are you helping your team stay within their window of tolerance?

Chapter 7 – Transforming School Culture

How do you move from isolation to collaboration?

- What are your team's "five words" for culture?
- What's one thing you can do this week to create connection?

Chapter 8 – Gratitude as the Fuel for Connection

How do you lead with thankfulness?

- What are three ways you've seen gratitude shift the tone in your building?
- Who needs to hear "thank you" from you today?

Chapter 9 – Lead with Love. Fuel with Joy.

How is joy showing up in your leadership?

- What traditions, routines, or surprises bring life to your staff?
- How can you be more intentional about leading with both love and laughter?

Chapter 10 – Start in the Parking Lot

What does community leadership look like for you?

- What assumptions might you or your team hold about families?

- How can you build trust outside of the school walls this month?

Chapter 11 – Beginning Again
What new beginning are you being called into?
- What shift is your team ready for?
- How can you model vulnerability and clarity in a season of transition?

Chapter 12 – Finding the Good
Where are you finding the good—even in hard places?
- What moments of joy, humor, or hope carried you recently?
- How do you help your team find and name the good?

Chapter 13 – Change Is Hard, But You Were Built for It
How do you navigate resistance and lead through discomfort?
- What's your "why" behind a change you're leading?
- What stage of change is your team in now—and how will you support them?

Chapter 14 – The Data-Driven Leader
How do you make data feel human?
- What story is your data telling—and what story do you want it to tell?
- How can you make data more accessible, actionable, and affective?

Chapter 15 – Servant Leadership: Empowerment Without Burnout
Are you helping or over-functioning?
- What do you need to let go of to lead more sustainably?
- How can you stretch your people instead of rescuing them?

Chapter 16 – The "Kids First" Philosophy

Are kids at the center of every decision?

- What system currently prioritizes adult comfort over student needs?
- When in doubt—how do you return to your compass?

Chapter 17 – Growing New Leaders

What legacy are you living now?

- Who are you mentoring right now?
- What seeds of leadership are you planting in your people?

Chapter 18- The Soundtrack of Your Legacy

What's your leadership anthem right now?

- When was the last time you paused to reflect-intentionally?
- What message do you most want to leave behind?

Epilogue – Stay the Course (Even If You Drew It Yourself)

What is your leadership soundtrack right now?

- What would your leadership legacy statement say?
- What message do you most want to leave behind?

Selected References

Brown, B. (2018). *Dare to Lead: Brave Work. Tough conversations. Whole hearts.* Random House.

Coyle, D. (2018). *The culture code: The secrets of highly successful groups.* Bantam Books.

Forbes, H. (2012). *Help for Billy: A beyond consequences approach to helping challenging children in the classroom.* Beyond Consequences Institute.

Korb, A. (2015). *The upward spiral: Using neuroscience to reverse the course of depression, one small change at a time.* New Harbinger Publications.

Payne, R. K. (2005). *A framework for understanding poverty* (4th ed.). Aha! Process, Inc.

Robbins, M. (2022). *The Let Them Theory.* [Podcast Episode/Online Resource].

Siegel, D. J. (Referenced in the Window of Tolerance theory).

Knight, J. (Referenced regarding instructional coaching and intentional dialogue).

Fullan, M. (2014). (Referenced in discussions on clarity and coherence in change leadership).

Scriptures and faith reflections throughout this book are drawn from the author's spiritual journey.

Personal Acknowledgements

Mr. Wilson – Thank you for seeing leadership I me long before I ever did. Your belief lit the first spark.

Mr. Decker – Thank you for handing me the keys to my first principalship and showing me what trust really looks like in action.

Mrs. Osborne – Our beloved counselor, your presence, your heart, and your legacy continue to ripple through everything I do..

Mrs. Kilby – Your joy is contagious, your laughter unforgettable, and yes- your squeaky cart was part of the magic that moved our culture forward..

To the teachers and students who've shaped how I lead—you've been my greatest teachers, whether you knew it or not.

And to my leadership teams—thank you for building alongside me, for the honest conversations, the deep dives into data, the visioning sessions, and the shared commitment to doing what's best for kids

Books, Articles, and Authors Referenced

1. **James Clear**
   - Quote: "In times of crisis, we don't rise to the level of our goals—we fall to the level of our systems."
   - Book: *Atomic Habits*
2. **Heather T. Forbes**
   - Concept: "Window of Tolerance" and trauma-informed strategies
   - Book: *Help for Billy: A Beyond Consequences Approach to Helping Challenging Children in the Classroom*
3. **Dr. Dan Siegel**
   - Concept: "Window of Tolerance"
   - Book: *The Whole-Brain Child*
4. **Brené Brown**
   - Quote: "Clear is kind. Unclear is unkind."
   - Concepts: Vulnerability, clarity, and trust in leadership
   - Book: *Dare to Lead*
5. **Jim Knight**
   - Concepts: Instructional coaching, active listening, and partnership in leadership
   - Book: *The Impact Cycle*
6. **Michael Fullan**
   - Concepts: Shared clarity, coherence, and collective efficacy
   - Book: *The Principal: Three Keys to Maximizing Impact*

7. **Alex Korb**, PhD
   - Concept: Brain science of gratitude
   - Book: *The Upward Spiral*
8. **Daniel Coyle**
   - Concept: Belonging cues, culture-shaping leadership
   - Book: *The Culture Code*
9. **Stephen R. Covey**
   - Concepts: Intentionality, proactivity, and values-based leadership
   - Book: *The 7 Habits of Highly Effective People*
10. **Tom Peters**
    - Quote: "Leaders don't create followers. They create more leaders."
11. **Mahatma Gandhi**
    - Quote: "Be the change you wish to see in the world."
12. **Helen Keller**
    - Quote: "Alone we can do so little; together we can do so much."
13. **Simon Sinek** (Indirectly)
    - Concepts around purpose, why, and leadership philosophy
    - Book: *Start With Why*